BDSM

I0088497

BDSM Guide

A BDSM Book, An Introduction To The Lifestyle

By

Katya Roberts

ALL RIGHTS RESERVED. This book contains material protected under International and Federal Copyright Laws and Treaties.

Any unauthorized reprint or use of this material is strictly prohibited. No part of this book may be reproduced or transmitted in any form or by any means, electronic, mechanical or otherwise, including photocopying or recording, or by any information storage and retrieval system without express written permission from the author.

Copyright © 2017

Published by: Zoodoo Publishing

Table of Contents

Introduction

You may have thought about some kind of kinky spices for your relationship, but you never explored the absolutely new world of kink. Maybe you're not kinky at all and you enjoy your everyday life, but just want to find out what's out there that makes people change their lifestyles for good.

BDSM isn't something you should be ashamed of, it's our society. People have had sex since the very first day of the world, and yet it's still a taboo just like BDSM.

In order for you to love it or hate it, you must educate yourself about it in order to make that decision. Through this book, you'll realize so many ways of use for BDSM that has nothing to do with roughness or someone being tortured against their will. You'll find out how to play with your partner in such innocent ways for you to keep that spark up between you and if and when you're ever ready, there are many other options to choose from.

For some, BDSM is all about authority-based relationships and who can give what and what to expect back. Others know better. Others know that BDSM is all about intensifying your sex drive along with your partner. Trying new things in order to experience new ways to enjoy life and therefore explore your sexuality and finally get a different kind of orgasm is something we should all do.

But before you enter this world, make sure you know what you want from it. Some get a completely different view of the world, some just seek advice and some are so familiar with this that they're reading in hopes something new has come up. See, as normal as it is to all of us to have sex, to the BDSM community it is too, but only with their own game rules. There's nothing wrong about that.

The only reason that people are refraining themselves from trying BDSM is because they're taught that it's wrong from media and/ or their community. They're aware that it's a taboo and are holding on to their inhibitions, while in fact, they should let them go and finally start growing as a person – whether it's BDSM or anything else sexual. Now is the right time to change that. So, let us begin.

Chapter 1. Quick BDSM quirks

New age world of stress has taken up so much of our lives in many aspects. You might agree without second guessing what those things are. Let's revise – your health, your self-esteem, your willingness to try new things that seem to pop up every single day just because you're not 20 anymore, sense of being close to someone since phones and technology, in general, are making us more distant and cold. What about you? What about what you want? Your whole life seemed to be planned out and achievements aren't fun anymore. Nothing seems to work to light that spark up in your eyes. You've seen all these kinky things and wanted to know what it's like, how do those people use all kinds of sources and things to spice up their love life?

Those who enter abandon all socially acceptable stigmas

50 Shades of Grey really kicked the stigmatic belief of people that the sex that we see on movies, series and in real life is all there is to it. Thanks to the movie, many people started finally talking about BDSM and exploring the world of BDSM and themselves. As you may recall, many were disgusted (at least that's what they acted out in public) and harshly commented the very thought of a movie like that being shown in theatres and having that huge marketing that tickled people's imagination.

A Refusal to be Labelled

Institute of Clinical Sexology in Rome, published a study that proved how those who practice BDSM are more satisfied with their love life and life in general, and how their sexual preferences have nothing to do with their everyday jobs and general contact with other people. People seem to think that having specific sexual preferences that may include having a life in a BDSM community makes you aggressive and unresponsive to your partner's needs, or even a bully who harasses a partner for selfish reasons and needs – leaving a deep psychological impact on a partner.

On the contrary, people that are aware of BDSM rules and communities, and have some BDSM experience, would tell you that that harassing your partner in any way that worsens person's health, especially without a consent- is absolutely forbidden.

BDSM 101: Abbrevations and their Meanings

BDSM (Bondage, Discipline, Dominance, Submission, Sadomasochism) or bondage is a term whose meaning could be described as giving and receiving sexual pleasure through the dominance of one person and obedience to another. This type of sexual expression is based on the voluntary attitude, safety and mutual trust of all participants and, ultimately, on receiving and giving pleasure.

Until recently, the notion of "bondage" was associated with something perverse, strange and nasty in popular culture and our society, but then came the book that changed everything - 50 Shades of Grey. Since then bondage and other "kinky" sexual practices have become mainstream - and there is a different sexual revolution going on. It becomes acceptable and common to talk about how we like to be spanked on the ass or to try out bondage.

This "vanilla" bondage may be miles away from what the "true" members of the BDSM community see, but there is no "real" and "guilty" bondage. It is the one that suits you and what your partner and you are creating and wanting it to be. Everything that is safe and on which you previously agreed on and with which you feel comfortable is all right.

Bondage can shake up sexual monotony, add a completely new dimension to good sex, or allow us to get to know our partner again and create an entirely new relationship with them. By letting ourselves experience this, we can get to know ourselves better through bondage, and find out why something, for example, is turning us on, or why we are being turned on in a certain way.

Let's first meet with the terms that appear in BDSM or bondage. Even though theory might bore you, it's crucial in order for you to know what you want and what you want to try out. Educating yourself first is a huge first step towards great sexual experiences.

BDSM is an abbreviation that in six words describes a sex world in which discipline, domination, and subordination are golden options from which you can choose or mix with one another, within which the game of play and humility is played, with the aim of experiencing pleasure.

B / D (bondage / discipline) refers to attachment and discipline, and the basic meaning of bondage is to achieve control and domination.

D / S (domination / submission) or domination versus subordination.

S / M (sadism / masochism) is the abbreviation for the pleasure of giving pain (sadism) and recieving pain (masochism). In this sense, in the BDSM relationship, one of the participant's pleasures is pain relief and the other receiving or pain endurance.

Dominance - is absolute control over another person, unquestionable governance, action and decision-making.

Submissiveness - or subordination is a complete abandonment of the dominant person and its demands, actions and desires.

Sadism - experiencing pleasure through the infliction of pain.

Masochism - the opposite of sadism, experiencing pleasure through receiving and enduring pain.

Bonding - is one of the forms of physical restriction followed by the various activities that the dominant person implements over a submissive person in order to achieve mutual pleasure.

Spanking - is an action that refers to hitting yours or partners ass with your hand, but spanking can also be done with some other objects (whips) across various parts of the body.

After a quick look at abbrevations and meanings, it's time for the fun theory part.

Chapter 2. Just let go

When you start to explore BDSM, remember that there's no need to dive right in to create your own "Red Room of Pain" like in the previously mentioned movie. For a start, you can simply try being blindfolded and get tickled by your partner with a feather, or spanked on your skin with a whip. If it turns you on, you can move towards to a bit racier bondage play, like binding wrists with handcuffs or a tie (or whatever does the job), or just exploring the sensation of spanking more but now in a more playful manner.

If you really want to go into BDSM seriously, you have to come up with boundaries beforehand with your partner before your sexy session. It's okay to use words in order to communicate when things get a bit too rough for you or just aren't doing the work for you, so a simple let's pause, or stop should be okay to say – just remember that everything you guys want to try out has to be spoken of before.

This will make you feel safe and therefore you'll have some control during this absolutely new experience. If your partner hasn't even come around to the idea of BDSM, start by talking figuratively about it. For example, discuss who would have to play the dominant and submissive roles, and be subtly clear about what you're willing to try since it's a new thing to him/her and what's really outside of your comfort zone.

After having this talk, you will know where you stand and it will strengthen your communication, build intimacy, and make a strong sense of trust, which means you can let go of your inhibitions and explore yourself and sex in some kinkier sex play in the safety and comfort of your own relationship.

It is okay to be submissive, but there must be consent

BDSM has become a wide network of countless possibilities and activities. From simple spanking and bondage to dominance, and even needle play, and beyond, it's easy to get overwhelmed when you first begin to explore this absolutely new world. At first, you'll have that feeling like you've been in a cage and you're finally free to do anything and the realization of that can make you feel like a little kid that was given a whole new range of candy possibilities to choose from.

Many people who are brand new to BDSM want to immediately try all the things all at once and end up burnt out from all the desire so they don't even get to the part of enjoying it. Just take it slow, you have to know that there will be endless temptations and that you'll have to have fun in a smart way. Remember consent! Consent, consent, and did someone say consent? If you focus only on yourself, there is no chance you'll enjoy any scene or act - you MUST start there, consent is everything and harassing your partner and pushing them into something they're not comfortable with is not only illegal but will affect you and them in more ways than one.

The whole idea of BDSM is based on a very important concept. If you avoid the rules of it, it means you risk doing significant harm to others – and that's a hard place to get out of once you go there, there's simply no going back to how it used to be once you abandon the needs and safety of your partner. Just remember this, his or hers consent must be willingly given, informed, and with full awareness and enthusiasm.

Have fun while playing

Feeling silly and awkward when you engage in your first few times of BDSM lifestyle is normal. It's okay, you're going to make some mistakes. BDSM is all about having fun while playing and exploring new parts of lust and desire and all of the fantasies. Keep up with the whole notion of having an adventure. Keep in mind that many BDSM activities can be and/or are dangerous, so find someone that can be your educator (this might terrify you or make you feel ashamed for asking something that now seems natural to that person, but it's okay – note that all of them were taught, nobody knew anything by simply being born) and ask for their help.

Note that if you're about to do a power play (Dominance and submission or Master and slave or Sadist and masochist), both of you actually have equal power when you talk beforehand about the activity. You decide the outline for how things are about to be done, especially at the very start. As you get better and better at arranging and negotiating a scene, you'll unleash your true potential on how to make it extremely sexy and even a great part of your foreplay.

Honesty is a really important aspect of BDSM. Your partner(s) need to know at least some basic information about you when it comes to past experiences, health issues, what triggers you emotionally, and absolute turn-offs. Don't expect that your partner can read minds and to know by default what your needs, wishes, and limits are. If the person that you are about to engage in BDSM activities with isn't asking you these questions, make sure you speak your mind and tell them how things are about to go down.

Chapter 3. Game Rules

Some S / M see it as a kind of theatrical play. Although BDSM relationships are submissive, this does not mean that they are necessarily such in real life. For some, Dom or Sub is actually a role, and for some of them it's a lifestyle – the latter BDSMs rarely see it as the kind of theater play, but we will stay on the terminology for a bit.

Scene and negotiation

The scene is the active time of the BDSM "session". BDSM activities usually take place over a period of time agreed on by both parties. This time can be called "game", "scene" or "session". The scene often has a moment "for itself" in which the Dom takes a break and talks with the Sub about what was good and what was not. Beginners in S / M would definitely have to use the ability to pre-arrange the structure of their first scene before the beginning.

After the end of the scene, take the time to discuss how the scene affected both of you. Listen to your partner and learn how he/she felt, and thank your partner for the game. After the scene, this is a really nice way to finish your meeting. This S / M negotiation concept simply means an open, honest communication about what you have done and about what you want or do not want to do. Negotiating in this sense is not a negotiation where one person wants to get something at the expense of the other; this is a technique where both talk about what excites you and what not.

Please, keep in mind that the BDSM is a game (although sometimes it may not seem like it) of mutual trust and appreciation.

Creation of a safe word

Some of the excitement of BDSM lies in the fact that you can examine and expand your limitations. If you enjoy this kind of game, you can naturally find yourself in a position to want more and more new things, accepting an ever-increasing level of sensation, working and feeling better than you ever have. This process is light and gradual; remember that people are not usually telepaths. It can happen that you are a Sub in the scouring scene and suddenly it does not seem pleasant to you anymore - you want your Dom to STOP. A safe word means - please stop. The safe word must be taken seriously.

It's good to use colors sometimes:

- *YELLOW* - which means - something is exaggerated, I want you to go a bit easier, but I do not want to interrupt the scene.

- *RED* - I'm in trouble and I want to stop everything immediately.

If the Dom person does not want to listen to a safe word, it is certain that he will not respect any other sub-restrictions. The Subs who take care of their health should avoid that type of Dom. Some Doms deliberately try out the very limit of Sub until a safe word is used in order to increase the Subs limits of endurance. Sometimes the Sub will have a clogged mouth, either because it was noisy or in order to increase the feeling of helplessness.

In such cases it is still possible to use the old SOS signal, three short shouts, three long and then three short ones again. Not all S / M players use a safe word. Some do it because of the style of playing, or a good negotiation phase, or have been with their partner for so long that he/she fully understands Sub-limits.

Basics of Safe SM, SSC vs. RACK

Some BDSM fans prefer a code of conduct that is different from a safe word and they describe it as "Risk Aware Conscious Kink" (RACK), which could be a style upgrade that emphasizes the individual responsibility of the parties involved. RACK does not focus primarily on consciousness and informed consent but relies on the principle implication of security arising from practice. Consent and approval are the most important criterion.

SSC refers to Safe, Sane and Consensual. Meaning that all BDSM activities should be safe, you should be in a sane and sensible state of mind and that all actions must be consensual. These rules are also something to keep in mind.

For their consent, there must be all the relevant information (to what extent the potential risks will be in the scene, whether to use a safe word - what he/she wants). The result, consent, approval, and understanding can often be summarized in the "contract", an agreement on what is acceptable, and what not in any future relationship among the partners to the participants.

It should be noted that this "contract" is purely symbolic in nature and has no legal weight. Infinite broad and gloomy discussions with the equally valid arguments of the opposing sides are conducted about the necessity/purpose of the existence of a contract in the BDSM communities.

An S / M game that includes helplessness, intense sensation, and psychological domination is a fatal thing - it can go deep into someone's soul and draw back the traumatic trauma of childhood or hidden fears - without warning. The person's Dom should be aware that they may be swimming in deep waters of a personal history without even knowing it, so be careful, kind and behave with respect to the Sub partner.

And part of the responsibility lies on the shoulders of Subs. Be honest. If you do not want to do something, do not let the partner force you to do it. When practicing S / M, you can often find yourself in a situation where a partner is looking for something that you do not want or cannot do. In this case, it is best to discuss and explain to your partner why you do not want to do so. Being in a scene you do not want to be in can lead, at least, to the feeling of discomfort, if not worse.

Do not be afraid to slowly explore, so gradually get to what your partner wants from you - but not by any means of force. If you are the Dom, keep your attention on what you are doing. Although the position of the Sub is to please you, it is up to you not to ignore the needs of your, at this point, slave. Fun cannot become boring, you always have to be on top of your game as much as you can and so does your Sub, and if you get bored doing things in one way, try another.

Chapter 4. DIY Dungeon

You might have a public dungeon in your home town but wouldn't it be better to have your own DIY dungeon within the walls of your own home, tailored to fit your particular kinks down to every possible fiber of your sexuality? It might seem like a really expensive wish or depend on where you live. It could be utterly impractical since you haven't got that much space, to begin with. Still, no matter what you say you have in terms of a budget and/or available space, you can make your own BDSM dungeon without becoming a burglar of the bank.

First and foremost, you should get a strong means of restraining your Sub. That shouldn't be a problem. Even if you don't have much space to spare, you can get sturdy hooks and screw them into the walls and ceiling and you can get them from any hardware store. There are heavy duty planter hooks or you can just buy anything that has a high weight tolerance and it will work like a charm, and from that point on, it's easy to sling ropes or manacles from these well-made fixtures, that way you'll ensure that your slave will be held properly.

There are other things you can try out too, those may include racks and cages in order to restrain your slave. Browse some yard sales and thrift shops in your surroundings. You can actually find a good bed frame that can be modified into a rack with a few 2 X 4s. Pet cages can be used too, those for larger dogs can make marvellous holding cages if your slave has been bad.

You probably already have a really great assortment of kinky sex toys and equipment which you use to punish your Sub, but you'll want and need a handy place to store them and always be ready to use them. You don't want to want to run through a box full of things trying to find that special toy, you can actually affect the mood of the foreplay by stalling. Put some pegboards on your walls and make certain sections for specific toys so you'll always know where things are at any given time when it comes to your instruments of punishment.

You might also think that you want some additional options in your bedroom. One product that is most popular with couples is the Liberator Wedge, which allows you to do some really fun and engaging positions, but you will still feel comfortable. You can also buy the Liberator Wedge/Ramp combination if you're into more versatility for the bedroom. Liberator Wedge is really comfortable and can come in different colors and shapes. You can always look it up online to find the perfect one for you in your area.

Adding some new furniture that can even be bought in second-hand shops might be a great thing. You may ask why? Well, you could buy an ottoman, which can be big enough to position you or your partner in many ways, and on the plus side, they almost always have hidden storage where you can put all your toys. Convenient isn't it?

Of course, it wouldn't be a great dungeon if things were too safe and sound. In addition to some nice furnishings, your dungeon needs to have some things that are designated to cause pain. At the very least, you need something to form any kind of restraints. At the bare minimum, you need some wrist restraints. If you're up for even kinkier things, you might want something even wilder, therefore you could try out a spinning sex swing.

Even if you aren't that crafty, you're going to make a really impressive dungeon of your own with almost no money. Plan things in advance, watch out for bargains, and in no time you'll have your dungeon before you even know it.

Relationship disclaimer

Like in BDSM, you both have to have a say on how the dungeon should be done. It might be excruciating at first since you two might not have the same taste in decorating the space, but see it as a great way to bond (this time not using bondage, only spiritually and emotionally folks!).

There are so many people in the BDSM community run blogs and guides in which they write articles about where to find some of the best tools and equipment for the lowest price in order to make your own dungeon a dream come true. If you're not sure how it will work and you two aren't that crafty, you can always follow Youtube instructions by Morgan Thorne, where she creates many how-to videos and is a part of the BDSM community itself.

Chapter 5. Never Ending Role Play of S&D

BDSM is a form of consensus roleplay between two or more individuals who use their pain and strength experiences to create sexual tension, satisfaction and / or freedom. BDSM encompasses a wide range of activities, forms of interpersonal relationships, and various subcultures. Many of these experiences still fall into unconventional sexual activity and human relationships.

One good option is to have a lot of hot sex. The second possibility is that the Dom somehow binds the Sub, which directly and physically brings the Sub into addiction and puts it at the mercy of the Dom, which then plays in order to achieve a mutual satisfaction. This is a game of bondage and supremacy/dominance (B / D). Some people enjoy punishing games, which is enjoying tying and discipline (B / D).

Then there is a kind of game called S / M - sadism and masochism. Whips, rods, nipple clamps and all those wonderful things that are made to cause pain. It can be a powerful thing to be submissive to someone who wants to hurt you; it's a fantastic expression of trust. As it will be explained later, pain is not really pain. In S / M games, pain becomes an intense stimulation that can subside to a whole new peak of ecstasy.

Activities and relations within BDSM are characterized by the fact that participants are usually complementary parties and their roles are unequal. Typically, participants who are active - by acting or exercising control over others - are known as top or Dominant. Those who are recipients of the activity or who are under the control of their partners, are usually known as bottom or Submissive. Individuals who are changing from a top / dominant role to a bottom / submissive role - occasionally within a relationship or from a relationship to a relationship - are known as switches.

It is this fundamental difference from the conventional one in which quality is regarded as equal to the partners of the relationship BDSM makes it attractive - the foundation of the BDSM relationship is based on the premise of deliberately unequal roles within the relationship.

Possible Dom-Sub rules

Trust, being careful, mutual agreement, safe sex practices, and safety, in general, are a definite must. Here are some guidelines regardless of what turns you on or not, it's suggested that you try to embrace the following and make a safe lifestyle because of it:

Please, don't tie things around someone's neck to the point where a person can't breathe. That's not sexy, that's harassment! The safe word has been mentioned before, so hopefully, there's no point on emphasizing it once again. Always be alert when you're about to engage in BDSM lifestyle, especially if you're a newbie. Educate yourself as much as you can and keep proper medical facilities handy. Always make sure that a Sub has never been restrained to the point where his/hers life is in danger.

If the person in bondage has any problems or just wants to go to the bathroom or make a call, that person has to be instantly released and set free from the bondage. Once again, make sure you know the medical history of the partner and create a BDSM session accordingly to it. Make sure to never leave anyone alone while in bondage, serious things can happen within seconds so you must always be on hand when playing a role of Dom.

Play with a ball gag beforehand with your partner so you can distinguish noises of pain, pleasure or any other for that matter. Please, never engage in BDSM sessions while using any kind of drug or alcohol for that matter, it can be dangerous as it is without someone being under the influence of these. Always make sure that both your handcuffs and lock keys work beforehand since the trip to locksmith won't be half as fun as the session itself.

When you are about to remove the partner from bondage, let them move their limbs per their wish. If you have a disability, or you're ill or better yet pregnant you'll need to check with your doctor before stepping into a BDSM session or activity. At all times be aware of your possibilities and skills, and never do anything that causes you discomfort.

The next section is a transcript by one of the frequent consumers of BDSM lifestyle, and it's written only as a pure guideline for imagination purposes – therefore, everything that is written shouldn't be used as a universal agreement upon BDSM sessions but rather to make you think of your rules of the game.

Life choice called Domme/Dominatrix

If you have ever done any research of your own concerning BDSM, then you must've come across these names. A Dominatrix is a woman that takes over the dominance in a sexual relationship with her partner. Her role of dominating can be also her sexual preference and orientation but it's not a must. She performs all sorts of treatments on her submissive, but all according to their previous agreement.

A Dominatrix is usually a well-paid professional that gets in contact with her clients that are looking for the experience that she offers with a mix of their own preferences. A Domme is just a male version of a Dominatrix. Some rely on all kinds of sites that provide a list of Dominatrix and/or Dommes that are available for you, of course for a certain price. Many go to the sites 'Kink Academy' and 'Fetlife' to find someone who will fulfill their needs or just to find out what's going on near them in the BDSM world so they can check it out.

Since it's, let's say global, you can't find an excuse not to get involved in any way, being it just going to a BDSM conference or actually finding a perfect fit for your sexual tensions.

Being and playing with a Domme/Dominatrix is all about safety. You should always keep that in mind since we all know BDSM can go over board when it comes to rougher sex and erotic play. SSC and RACK are two fundamental beliefs of the BDSM community for you to follow and forever to have in mind when engaging in a session. BDSM can be used in many different ways for many things, but some people have problems differentiating play for the real world and sometimes they even manifest their sexist, oppressive or violent beliefs.

It's really good to examine yourself before engaging in an activity that may or may not draw out the worst in you, which you might not be even aware of. Check your biases and privileges and realize what's a downfall to your personality due to not being informed enough or just misinformed. Even though punishment can be a part of BDSM, abuse is never a part!!! Abusers can be kinksters too, but that doesn't mean that all kinksters are abusers. Please note the differences.

Keeping SSC and RACK in mind, being aware of what you're interested in and what the limits are for you and your partner(s) will help you in having a good time when you do engage in a session or a scene. Sometimes scenes can involve multiple people, and roles might be fixed, but not necessarily.

Ground rules before engaging

Talk with your (sex) partner about things like what kind of play you are both interested in. What types of entertainment are on the table? Always define what is okay with you and if there are any possible exceptions (aka soft limits), and what's definitively out of the picture (aka hard limits) and then make sure you stick to that list. Use really detailed Want, Will, Won't lists and a BDSM Checklist as a starting point with your (sex) partner.

Please note that you cannot try something out if it wasn't arranged beforehand even if it isn't on your partner's No list. It's normal to list the things you enjoy or hate but many forget to include anything they're unsure of or haven't tried yet or are willing to if asked. After the scene is finished, you must discuss what worked for both of you, what didn't, and possibly think of some ideas for the next try that you might have thought of during the act.

Dialogue

The talk about ground rules should include the way you speak to and about each other, what terms to use and when. Sometimes people just crack up at the very thought of some words, let alone of using them. Make a list of words and things you can't say to avoid this problem. It is a great way to make sure you're both on the same level when it comes to levelling degradation (if any) your sub prefers, and how you'll flow with each other. Many forget that people are human beings and that everyone has their own background, so going over a list of words that are an absolute no is a great way to eliminate the risk of triggering someone's bad memories.

Walk towards it with simplicity

Keep it simple. Before doing something you might regret due to dishonesty to your partner, which is common, you have to be honest with yourself and then take into account your partner about your BDSM experience and limits or lack of them. Even though this is probably boring you, there's nothing more painful than a BDSM session gone bad – especially those that could've been prevented with a simple TALK, and that's way more important than being considered as a BDSM expert. Start off with a simple scene that includes kinks you're more comfortable with and then slowly but surely build up to more advanced acts. It takes time to learn limits each other's limits, but researching techniques/safety precautions and talking to other people in the community about it will help you to avoid rush into things and to go too far too quickly since you might just go over your head.

Face and body recognition

Partners can tell when someone is going through pain, discomfort or anything that makes them feel bad just by looking or listening to their partner. Sure, this comes from experience, but sometimes even with it, it's hard to tell let alone without it so when not sure feel free to ask your partner what they're thinking. Don't think of it as a mood killer, you can still ask away without ruining the scene and the tone of the scene while still being in character. There are plenty of ways to do so.

Experience richer by every practice

Domination has to do with performance as much as it has to with eroticism. Even though there are some characteristics of how one should act, the truth is that the domme and dominatrix role varies by person and have to do much more with their original character and preferences. There are so many approaches that you can try, from really polite demands to consensual but completely degrading commands. No matter the personality of the domme and dominatrix and their feelings towards the sub, the more plays you have the more you enjoy playing and staying in your act. You may also realize that your style changes depending on the person you're playing with in a certain session.

Watching some BDSM pornography might be helpful when it comes to a technical point of view. The dynamics between individuals is unique, so please be aware that not everything that was shown on BDSM pornography is equal to your or your partner's limits and skills, and also (same as vanilla pornography) it doesn't depict the real truth and don't use it as the only source of BDSM sex education.

Some are more prone to being a Domme or Dominatrix, but one should also try being a sub just to see how it goes and to realize from that position how to improve the next scene when the roles are switched again. Being submissive may not be the best thing in the world to you and it isn't required for being a good domme, but it sure can give you a new perspective. However, finding an experienced mentor can help you learn dominant tips and tricks way more quickly than you would by yourself.

Basics covered, what now?

Now that we've covered how to be a domme for personal reasons in the comfort of your partner's arms, let's go over how to make this a hobby of your own or even your job if you're interested enough. For some, professional domination is a very dreamy career where you get to set your own hours and work for yourself. Even though sexual acts or contact isn't a must of being a pro-domme, it's just usually considered as sex work in the eyes of the law, though it might vary from state to state, sometimes even from town to town. Sometimes being a domme (or "dominatrix," - that is usually the term given to people who are in the business "professionally") isn't really illegal, it's at the discretion of local law enforcement to handle the prostitution laws and decide for themselves whether to prosecute or not in times of need.

So before you get your first client, try to get to know your basics. I can't tell you the every detail since the laws vary but I hope to get you in the right direction to do so yourself.

Do your homework

Find out the laws in your state and city when it comes to domination and prostitution. Some cities and states have well-defined legislation written for both while others are more open to interpretation. Inform yourself about these laws and get some advice from a kink- or sex-positive lawyer. They usually provide more detailed information about what you can and cannot do to while working and much more. On the Kink Academy site there's a section for legal concerns and they have a detailed listing of federal and state prostitution laws and penalties.

Check out your competition, see what kind of domme and dominatrix there is and what are they offering so you can cover your information basis. There's a lot to choose from: impact play, degradation, ageplay, foot worship, medical play, and electrostimulation – these are just some of activities a pro-domme can specialize in. Some focus on just one or a few things they specialize in, while others give a full spectrum of services. Find out what's hot in your area to which you can give your special mark and start off.

Do a research on where you'll work. Public dungeons are a great start. Some just are waiting for a client to call and do house visits, while others make their own home a dungeon of itself and make their clients come to them. SAAFE (Support And Advice For Escorts) is really a great organization where you can find out a lot about sex work and workers, but also how to work with clients in all kinds of locations. It is really crucial to use pseudonyms when going into business, especially if you're working from your home or renting a place to be with a client.

Kinks go above and beyond, so it's normal that some want more than one domme or dominatrix for a scene. If playing a multiplayer game is something you're into, then take some time to find another domme/inatrix you're comfortable working with, since that's a way better option than having someone forced on you to work with. Go over your domme/inatrix basics and usual plays so both can establish whose place is where. Once you get to the same page, make the ground rules with your possible client(s) for each individual before every scene. When there are more people involved, the more complicated the rules can get so you have to be cautious.

Pro tips and where to get them

BDSM classes and reads are great but if you're willing to make a career out of it, you must find a mentor. Visit a local club/dungeon, play party, conference or just search online to check if any dommes are up for taking on a brand new protégé. Not all dommes are really good at what they do, so make sure you check with others while chatting about their experiences and what not in order to find someone close to your own preferences and wishes of learning. Experienced dommes will be able to help you work on your technique for a spectrum of kinks and clients. A professional domme can give out important information about the business input of being a domme. It can be on how to advertise and find clients, taxes, local laws and law tips and tricks. When you learn from someone who's already out there in the industry, it can give your domme career a really good start and even better, a push. On the blog of Mistress Amanda Dwyer you can find a lot of personal information about being a pro-domme while on Dungeonnet's Distance Domination section you can find lists of sites that give out information on where to apply and find educational resources and training for newbies in Domme/inatrix world.

Soul in its right place

The same as with any other job, to become the best you have to love what you do and be ready to adapt to possible changes in the industry. Competition can frighten you and can be fierce in cities that have tons of dommes. Even though you'll set your own guidelines on what your specialty is or will be, your clients might approach you with kinks that might not appeal to you or you just haven't tried before. By educating yourself with a new range of kinks early—like watching another domme's session—you'll get a better view of things on what falls under the "Yes", "No", and "Depends on the client/scene" category. Be aware of your limits and stand by them.

Even if it sounds hard, many dommes wouldn't change their lifestyle or jobs for anything in the world since they enjoy their work so much, despite the fact that some might describe it as a difficult career path. In the end, you know yourself better than anyone and what will make you the happiest in life as possible. Sex work as a pro-domme can be a short term experiment or turn out to be a long term lifestyle. If you're curious enough to actually give it a shot, play smart, play safe and have fun while doing so.

Cock Worship – yes, it is a thing

Cock worshipping is, as the name says itself, any activity that's all about the submission and worship of a penis. Please note that while there are possibilities such as for a man to worship another man, or for either sex to worship a transsexual's penis, we'll just talk about the most common situation where a dom is a male and a sub is a female. In all cases, cock worship will be of the same nature and power exchange.

Due to the sexual nature of a man's penis, worshipping cock is really a common activity for female subs to engage in. Cock worshipping may involve many activities and range of activities that all lead to making the male feel powerful and really confident with his penis.

Much cock worship is wrapped around the personal desires of the submissive individual which they enjoy doing. Complementing the penis is also considered as a cock worship, with detail given on a focus to the size, thickness, and hardness of the dick that's being worshiped. In most cases, average-sized penises are still being complimented in the same fashion with a goal of having a great time on both parties' sides so therefore one must go out of the way to make the other feel worshiped.

Cock worship, when speaking of physical terms, is mostly engaged with the mouth and the hands. Licking, stroking, sucking, kissing and playing with the length of the penis are all ways with which a submissive individual can worship the cock that's in front of them.

Even though it is not always the case, worship of the testicles is also connected with cock worship as well, since some people use their mouth to pleasure a man's balls while giving them a handjob.

Subs, when it comes to cocks, will often consider the size and thickness to be the most important elements. Most females seek out men with large penises and submit to them, just because of the fact that they have a large one. In some instances, racial dynamics and worship of black men come into play, since black men are often thought to have larger penises than any other race out there. The phrase 'BBC worship', which means big black cock worship, is used in the situations to denote the desire of submitting to a black man.

For the worshipper of a cock, receiving cum is the ultimate goal. Bringing a man to a point where he's getting into a frenzy with pleasure is thought to be a big compliment and really pleasurable for those that worship cock.

Clothing and private time

The Dom is really the one who explores his/her kinks when it comes to clothing, but if anything is making the Sub uncomfortable – it has to go off the table. Different Doms, different game rules, but some tend to even call the shots for the Sub's clothing outside their dungeon. However, any kind of financial dependency isn't okay, where the other person has to become a slave for money purposes.

The rules of private times or alone times are simple – all of us have to take care of ourselves. So, which rules apply to this aspect mixed with the BDSM world? Doms usually come up with some of the rules like what bad habits are okay or not okay, since in a way, even though it's an act meant for a pleasure stimuli, the Dom has that responsibility to take care of the Sub and think in the best matter for him/her. However, as we have said, the Sub must always agree.

Privacy settings

Dom uses privileges of kissing his/her Sub any time he/she likes, except the beforehand made exceptions to the rule like for public occasions where the Sub may be ashamed to be kissed in front of family, friends or at work. In that case, it's absolutely forbidden to go against the rules and push someone to kiss you back or be kissed. Yes, you read it right – there has to be consent even for kissing! In private, the Dom can kiss away as much as he/she likes.

In the privacy of their own home or dungeon, the Dom is usually granted to remove clothing from the Sub. If the Sub is a woman, the Dom almost always puts down a rule of a clean pussy when interacting with its Dom. If it's not cleaned and refreshed, then the Sub can be punished. Not only does she have to take care of her hygiene but elasticity also, therefore she has to work out in order to keep the pussy tight.

For some, it's even a matter of pride to have a vagina as tight as possible since mostly they get rewarded for it. Some

Doms even give orders to their Sub of when to cum. There's even a name for it and it's "Orgasm on demand". It's not possible for newbies and has to be perfected by every session, so it takes time to get to that point where you can cum on the very demand of your Dom.

It's seen as a matter of pride, and the full notion of obeying to someone's needs and wishes. While on the other hand, if the Sub is a woman, she may never touch cock or the balls of the Dom without his say so.

The orgasming part of the Dom has to be respected, therefore the Sub has to make that moment special and if it's possible cum as hard and as loud he/she can.

When giving a blowjob to the Dom's cock, many insist on swallowing the cum and continuing going back to the blowjob waiting for another cum shot until the Dom says it's enough. Same goes for when a woman is a Dom. While some others, are not that into someone handling their weak spots after cumming since the tip of the cock gets really sensitive. If the Sub refuses to swallow the cum of his/hers Dom, he/she deserves to be punished.

The thrill of wanting to cum while being with your Dom or Sub has to be always present. So, the Sub, when in privacy with his/her Dom has to go down on his/her Dom really often. Some even clock their partners. The Dom always determines how often and long going down on one on other will be, unless there are things to consider such as sickness and things that cause discomfort.

Chapter 6. Order of restraint

It seems that we went over the basics of communication a thousand times, since you have to know all the quirks of your partner— so you can know what scares your partner on a very thought of it or what your partner would like to try out but is scared or just uninformed. If you're aware of all this it means you've already had the "what turns us on" conversation and have gone through the whole what should we try out, what seems interesting and what's a total no.

Now, down to mechanics. It might feel not that important when compared to embodying the Dom persona. It's really important for you to know that sometimes the Dom persona and mechanics go hand in hand and it's hard to differentiate it sometimes. So for the sake of you learning all the fun technical stuff the bondage world has to offer, let's go over a few things to start with.

Sext your way to bondage

It keeps your partner in the fantasy world so both of your imaginations get aroused and you get a pretty good insight on what works for you without that face to face awkwardness. It also gives you a huge amount of time to draft something up—it's okay if you can't think of anything special, maybe your partner takes time to light up to the very idea of sexting so you don't have much material to work with. You can send the first sext. If your partner responds well to some of them, you memorize it somewhere in the back of your mind and pull it right back up when it comes to game time. Here are a few ideas that you can work with and make your own:

-"degrading" nicknames (for example, " dirty little slut.") (Quotation marks are there since all of this goes under the consensual part, if this isn't something your partner is up for, then you'll have to abandon it and find something more fitting that will arouse your partner)

- not so degrading nicknames (for example, "my good little slut")

- all sorts of fun punishments for disobeying

- and fun punishments for being a good girl/boy

- leashes, collars and leather meant for playing

- asking/demanding permission

Meaning of a collar

It's generally believed that the idea of collar was stolen in one way by the BDSM community from cultures that historically would collar their slaves as a sign of their status, while other communities aka "Old Guard" claim that there were more systems for the collar use that were related to the system of education or experience and it all had to do with who wore which type of leather collar. Since the information and thoughts conflict, it probably wasn't that big of a deal until the moment the BDSM community took over.

Today, the collar can have a wide range of meanings and its appearance can also vary depending on the people using it. Some of the meanings say that it's similar in many ways to the idea of "the wedding ring". We see it in photos, we read of their excitement of the ones who've received or given one, and if we pay close attention, we might even be a little confused about what it really all means.

Unlike "the wedding ring", the collar doesn't really have a specific meaning. The idea of itself packs the same psychological and emotional process in some ways, but writing down just what it means is a lot more difficult. But even though there are some exceptions, the wedding ring is more to be understood to mean "legal and serious commitment to a long term relationship and partner" in some way.

Many just assume it means a wedding ring in a BDSM world, but it doesn't have to. Most importantly, it's really crucial for you to talk about the meaning of the collar with the collar giver since it can mean all sorts of things – everything is on a personal level, so any assumptions made towards people wearing collars are possibly wrong from the very start.

Some possible meanings of the collar and situations:

1. D/s Commitment: These symbolize a commitment for the partner using it. It might or might not have involved a proper "collaring ceremony".

2. Consideration: Sometimes a submissive that's been considered by a Dominant will wear the collar that's given to them. It can also go vice versa where Sub considers a Dom.

3. Play Collar: This one is used only during a specific scene that was beforehand planned out. It can symbol that the scene has begun, that they are currently in their acts, which means when they're not in the character the collar is off. As it says, it's used for playing and can be powerful when grabbing someone by it or just any other different play you have in mind.

4. Situational Collar: This one is mostly used for the short period of time, usually when there's a BDSM event and one wants to show they're taken or just out of bounds for engaging in any BDSM activity with anyone other than the one for who they wore the collar.

5. Identity Collar: Believe it or not, some people identify as a slave or just a sub for life, and therefore wear a collar as a signature. They can be single, available and/or looking for their Dominant partner.

6. Pet Play: Dog and cat collars are really a hit for those who like pet play.

There are of course other reasons for the use of collars, take fashion for example. In fact, many people nowadays are wearing "every day collars" now that chokers are in fashion and if you're in the BDSM community this might even confuse you. Now more than ever, when you're at a gathering of BDSM, leather or just kinky folks, you'll have to ask for the meaning since you can't be sure anymore. Most people that are wearing a collar are happy to tell you all about it and be admired for it.

So, basically don't assume that a really cool necklace is a collar, but don't assume otherwise either.

Etiquette?
Collars might call for a special etiquette in some circles. For example, in a partner relationship, if one is wearing a collar it's not that crazy to ask their partner if it's okay if you speak to them or if you do without asking and they don't reply don't be offended by it. Those are just their rules of the game.

If you're newbie to a group or a party, find out if there is a protocol rule to be followed and if there are any rules for collars or anything else, and what they are so you can follow. There will be some tools there to make them clear and people that will answer questions. Mostly if you're new they'll cut you some slack since it's hard to get by and get accustomed to the rules you're seeing for the first time so they'll even help you out with them. If they're being rude because you're not keeping up with the rules you just found out about, they're being jerks so just ignore it since no one was born to do everything and to know everything in this world.

Never assume

Even though this is right for most of your life in different life spectrums, we're just going to go over BDSM basics. The collar can be a powerful symbol; it can also be a convenient play toy. There isn't actually a right way to define what it means. As in vanilla life, giving a ring or whatnot can mean to the much more to the receiver and without speaking about it they can't know your point of view, same goes with collars – one can put a play collar on their partner and they can start thinking it means that they're committed to each other. It is whatever you want it to be.

Intro to bondage

Tying people up is fun and you'll see why and how.

Before any actual bondage starts, talk to your session partner about what you're about to do – a yes/no/maybe list can help. If you've never tied someone up or been tied up, you probably don't know how you will react or how someone else will, and that's okay since you have to slow down and check in often with your partner. The goal is primarily to have fun, but you need to stay safe, and everything has to be sane and consensual, and communication is important.

The best rope for bondage is thick cotton or silk since none of these can let anything slide or move around much once you tie it off. That kind of rope is a bit expensive though, so you have to be ready to really give out some money for a proper rope. Buy some solid-braid nylon rope in 7/16" or 3/8" in diameter from any basic hardware store. Compared to any other types of rope, these knots will stay really easy to untie even after you pull them really hard, which is great for both partners.

Compared to the other types of toys, a rope is always multi-purpose. You can make your own DIY handcuffs (which will be explained further on), but not only that - you can also make a DIY flogger, strap-on harness and/or belt, and not to even begin with all the ways you can restrain someone.

Before diving right into the BDSM world out, please keep this in mind:

• You must keep the rope loose enough so that person has a good blood circulation and the only way to do so is if you can work two fingers between the rope and your session partner's skin. If the rope gets wet, you'll have to leave it even looser.

- A frequent check for skin discoloration is a must, please check at any possible time if the areas that are affected the most have any discoloration. Also, be kind enough to ask your session partner if everything is okay, do they feel numbness or pain, or pins and needles?

- Never be that person that ties someone in a way that they can't breath. It goes south very easily.

- Having someone tied up means you're the responsible person, you're in charge, therefore never leave someone alone who's tied up.

- At all times, keep scissors handy for times of need of quick release. Every second matters.

- There's nothing wrong with going slow, some even find it antagonizing but in a sexy way, like they have to earn it. Try something like just tying your partner's arms with ropes, police style. Add a bit of a role play and voila!

The following directions are for tying your partner's wrists together, but you could also try tying ankles together too, or wrists to ankles, or wrists and ankles to furniture. The wrap itself is really strong but leaves a lot of ways for you two to play and get your imagination going. Please note that these directions on tying are only for fun purposes and can be done only with the consent of your partner.

What you will need is 25 feet of rope, a partner that's all aboard with it or just some practice furniture for the learning phase and blunt edged scissors for worst case scenarios.

Tell your partner to have their wrists in front of them with at least two wrist sizes of space between them. Lay the rope over the wrists so the middle of the rope is strongly between their hands. Wrap every end around twice, then go for a total of five wraps. Cross the ropes beneath your DIY handcuffs. Then bring them up and around on the opposite sides from where they started (the back rope over the front and the front over the back).

Wrap up each end of rope all around, moving towards your partner's wrists. Stop winding it when you have a small gap between the wrapped rope and their skin. It should end up with an equal number of wraps on each side of the first crossed ropes. If it seems a little loose, twist both sides in the direction you wound it to tighten everything a bit. You might need to wrap both ends once a few times more after.

Pick up the last loop from the left side and tuck the end of the rope through the resulting circle from inside to out. Do it once more on the other side to tie everything off. Pull both ends of the rope to make it strong and more secure. You can either tuck in the remaining ends into the wrap (if they're shorter than expected), or you can use them to tie your session partner to some furniture or something else. And voila! You've made it!

Spanking and other assortments

Hands are something you're familiar with and fun and easy to control, so what about using yours. Focus on the fleshy areas of the body that are muscley and are prepared to absorb the impact, and you should most definitely avoid kidneys, tailbone, and hands and feet (so ass and thighs are probably a good spot to start from).

Start with lighter strokes and go to heavier ones as you guys warm up for the rest of the session. You can always try out: different positions, angles and toys (like paddles, floggers, and/or riding crops) diverse things can stimulate different sensors in both of you and it's the only way for you guys to know what arouses you and what doesn't. It's also fun to combine things together like strokes with some toys like nipple clamps.

Try not to buy leather wrist restraints the very first time you're about to tie your partner up, but it's possible that you own scarfs, ties, belts, or pantyhose, and almost every one of them can do the trick (and can be used as blindfolds). You definitely have ice cubes. Or maybe lotions that could work as a massage lotion. See, use of your hands is fun and you can get creative in more ways than one!

There are so many things you can also try out but some take some skills or are just there to spice things up a bit and are good for newbies, so here's a list:

- Bondage (light)
- Bondage (heavy)
- Bruises
- Corsets
- Cuffs
- Exhibitionism
- Food play
- Gender play
- Hair pulling
- Ice cubes
- Leather restraints
- Nipple play
- Orgasm denial
- Power play (all sorts of things)
- Spanking (giving)
- Spanking (receiving)
- Teasing
- Whips

.......and so much more, the limit is where your imagination ends. Discuss this with your partner. Keep your goal in mind: to be safe, sane, consensual, and there's only one way to do that - it is through honest communication.

Forced orgasm

It's as it sounds – really hardcore. Forced orgasms and involuntary orgasms are most often confused. On the surface, they might even seem the same, but they are really very different! Both of these involve having an orgasm in a bit of a struggle. One is fun and sexy, the other is a violation of a person and their body parts.

A forced orgasm is a type of play that's used in the BDSM community. It is used in a scene to give an individual an orgasm without their permission, but with their given consent. Usually, this is just a fun play between a sub and dom where the dom is trying to make the sub orgasm while the sub, even though he/she's restrained or whatnot, tries their best not to orgasm. The orgasm is there to be resisted, but the consent must be given for the orgasm to occur, so it's a true win-win for everyone involved. This is can also be referred to as "consensual nonconsent."

Typically, a scene where forced orgasm occurs involves bondage. The submissive is usually restrained at the wrists, ankles, and hips to prevent movement. Sensory deprivation like blindfolds is also commonly used to heighten the sensation of the play and the scene itself. Communication is the real key to finding out what the greatest way to make your partner cum is. When you find this out you can then use the information against them or for them!

Involuntary orgasms are sexual arousal and orgasms that happen when there's a forced sexual contact. It can happen to anyone regardless of the gender of the person that's involved. I want to highlight what I am about to say, this is so important for EVERYONE to know – when someone has an orgasm while being

51

raped IT'S NOT THEIR FAULT. No, they're not enjoying it, they're being traumatized. The body can't help itself by responding to external sexual stimulations and in no way possible does this mean that consent to any sexual assault was given by a person getting raped. Many of these situations go unreported because society is so into "slut shaming" and a pro at a "rape culture."

Ways to Force Orgasms

Forced orgasms aren't simply just for male Dominants/tops having climax after climax from their female submissive or bottom. People with penises are able to have their orgasms forced. Just be aware of the fact that no matter who you're playing with, the whole process and the time needed for it is going to be different for everyone, no matter the gender.

You might have a partner, male or female, who can achieve just one orgasm at a time. You can also have one who is multi-orgasmic, especially after their first climax. Take your time, take care your partner and be patient. The pleasure is in the process itself just as much as it is in the final outcome.

Bondage and Vibrator Play

You can do a quick image search for any type of forced orgasms and vibrators, and it's really likely you'll come across the iconic image that almost all kinksters know and love: a person that's bound with a rope and a really big vibrator attached to their genitals. Don't forget

- the bigger the vibrator (and its vibrations), the bigger and even more intense the orgasms.

You don't have to be an expert on tying the knots or be a personal Shibari expert for your partner to get a similar scene. Bondage tape, handcuffs, or silk scarves that can bind your partner to any flat surface, like a bed or the kitchen table, which are used the most, will do the job. Once you're assured your partner is properly tied, it's time to turn on the vibrator. Rope harnesses and tape are able to be attached or you can just stand and hold it against them.

Yes, penises enjoy vibrators as well. A penis can harden to steel, gets filled out with need and desire, and then is outed until the every drop of semen is out. Contrary to popular belief, some men are even capable of having multiple orgasms, although they still might need some time between each of their climaxes.

Forced Orgasms and masturbation

Forced orgasms don't have to be created just by your partner. You can do it yourself! Start by rubbing yourself. Let it build and accumulate. If it's possible, don't rush your first orgasm. Definitely don't stress out if it takes you a while to build. If you're away from your partner or even having a long distance relationship, use Skype or the phone to be together.

Once the first orgasm kicks in, keep moving your fingers or pressing your vibrator against your own body. Yes, even though it hurts. More than ever when it hurts. With that, you'll let your next orgasm build up through the very bottom of your feet and race up your legs. It's is truly an electrical jolt to your system. You might even want to close your legs and clamp down on your hand or toy – whatever you used. Sometimes just that makes it worse, so if you're trying your best to get away or rid of the sensations, it probably just won't help, but you'll definitively force at least one more orgasm in the same direction of that way.

The pain outweighs the pleasure. That will probably be after the second orgasm. Maybe even after the tenth. Move your hand away. Now you can enjoy your personal afterglow.

Chapter 7. Ways to Tie up Your Partner

Being new to all this, you should consider taking it slow and trying out the easier scenes that have less danger involved. When improving in the BDSM world, feel free to use other possibilities with great caution. Here are some ways to tie and be tied even for those who are gentle and fragile, and those who are afraid of nothing that's bestowed on them.

Classic Damsel

This position represents the classic damsel-in-distress of the silver screen. In the usual variant the elbows are tied touching each other behind the back, wrists are tied, and the legs are tied together above and below the knees as well as at the ankles. The elbows together produce a really tough tie and the shoulders-back position forces the person into a usual display of a Sub, emphasising the sexuality of the person itself. Even though the legs are bound together it deforms any other sexual activity, so this is considered a modest pose, usually used for display, teasing and punishment use.

Box Tie (Arm position), Frogtie (Leg position)

The box tie is basic for many bondage positions, restriction is made without causing discomfort or disrupting the blood flow and nerve issues in a way that the elbows-together tie often does. So, it is suitable for positions that take their time to tie, while elbow together positions should and are almost always limited to one of those where elbows can and usually are tied last and untied really really fast.

The shape is formed in a somewhat less pleasing way than the elbows-together tie to many eyes, but is very useful for the large number of combinations it allows. The ropes that go around the upper arms and chest are used to prevent the person from wriggling her wrists free of the tie at the small of her back; for more immobility this rope can be attached to a crotch rope.

This position combines the bow tie arm position with the frogtie leg position. Frogtie is a really vulgar and pretentious name for a most useful position – the leg is bent at the knee, and tied just below the knee and a bit above the ankle. This allows plenty variations in poses and a bit of mobility– it is truly impossible to stand up, or raise his/her head above a certain level, which can be used as a great feature of this tie. The humiliation part could be easily set by telling the Sub that the reward will be given only if she/he can reach a token placed at his/her normal head level – a place where it will be inaccessible, even if she/he has abilities of a ballerina.

The real use of frogtie is always sexual. Even though there are restrictions imposed by the tie, the person can open her/his legs widely and so can be taken in every desired angle.

Hogtie

The most known feature of the hogtie is the rope bounding the wrists to the bound ankles. This feature ensures that the hogtie manages maximal possible restriction for the Sub from minimal effort on the part of the captor. There are few ways of restraining someone effectively with really little rope for the basic hogtie

There are some positions that can be easily accomplished with metal, either with handcuffs and leg-irons (you only have to cross the chains linking the wrists and ankles) or with the shackles and chains. For this variation the name is a hogshackle. There are also bondage toys designed to hold the subject in a certain position and are generally called "hogties".

Mobility is almost always restricted to being able to roll over, and maybe from there being able to go up into a bridge position. The Sub mostly finds it more comfortable to be able to roll, since it relieves the pressure off the chest. If the hogtie is drawn really tight, even this amount mobility can usually be restrained to most Subs.

From an aesthetic aspect, it has the great advantage of displaying the best parts of the Sub simultaneously, and may be considered the bondage equivalent of "the pose" for those beloved foot fetish enthusiasts in the world.

Balltie, plus Legs Up-Balltie variant

There are many variations for the basic balltie theme. The basic similarity is that the knees are brought up to the chest and meant to remain there with rope. There's usually a use of a single cinched band of rope at breast level; this can be prone to some slippage if it isn't properly secured. Other variations bring the ropes over the shoulders, using the arms to prevent slippage.

The balltie is normally completed by binding the wrists and ankles. In the basic variation, these should be tied together but then additional rope should be used to draw the bound ankles in to the body to keep the knees bent, either by extending the chest band to wrap and cinch around the bent knees and shins or by adding rope to pull the ankles in, like to a crotchrope.

Tiptoe Crotch

This position is one of those that refers to any arm position where the arms are bound together behind the back and elevated, you know – police arrest style. It was and is used as a real-world torture position and therefore many are reluctant to use this very term, but it is so widespread in the world that it is unavoidable to use it. It is of a great importance to note that the leverage of the arms can in probably dislocate the shoulders and because of that you must be very careful when rigging the position. An attempt to suspend or semi-suspend any person by their arms is a tiptoe crotch!

The crotch rope is usually not attached to the rest of the bondage and serves basically as a decoration. The ankles are bound to a spreader bar, making sure they're far apart. The Sub is ordered onto her tiptoes and to remain there. Her/his elbows should be again bound together behind her back, which toughens the effect of the position. Her/his arms were bound to a hard suspension point, but a rope with reasonable stretch is used incase she/he slips or faints.

With all that said, this position is very eye pleasing, can be practical when properly used and allows the rearward penetration of the Sub.

Reverse Prayer (for arms) Karada/Tortoise-shell

This is one of the all time favourites when it comes to the decorative bondage, it can be tied by the Sub themselves after some basic training. Even though it's not being functional as a restriction, the rope web can provide anchorage for any number of other supplies and attachments, and does bring that east tradition to us along with the eye pleasing appearance to look at. If tied very tightly, it can also produce a really strong sensation, which some Subs find pleasurable.

The rope web can been used as an anchorage for the stripped-down form of the reverse prayer tie, which can then keep the hands and palms together behind the Subs back. There are many more secure variants of the reverse prayer tie but the variant that is explained is pleasingly minimalistic.

For the final look you can add some of the classic damsel positions, and nipple clamps added as a display and punishment measure. It is possible to make the same tortoise-shell effect down the legs too, proceeding in a usual manner to the way the tie is rigged on the body and making a visually pleasing.

Legs Up, Wrists to Knees

The legs-up position is of great use. When used with a spreader bar, it can be extremely conducive to face to face intimacy during sex, without the possibility of shyness. When used with ankles together, it provides the picture perfect target for the tie up. The degree of restraint produced is proportional to the height to which the Subs feet are raised. You have to be wary of raising the rope too high in order to avoid putting unbearable pressure on the back of the neck.

There are various ways in which the hands can be secured. They can be bound to the ropes around the knees, with the final knot tied behind the knees to be outside of finger reach. It can also be done very easily with the arms tied "hugging" the legs.

Yoke

It should also be achieved by using the ropes tied to a pole (the length of bamboo should be okay) although you should be careful if the pole is going to be attached at neck height – make sure there is no rope tied around the neck.

The yoke was featured in one of the BDSM-themed films called "The Secretary". The Subs fingers are free and unrestrained, so she/he can do usual chores and everyday life activities. However, the Sub can't get her/his hands near her/his mouth, therefore he/she cannot feed herself/himself easily.

It is usually used as the training aid, and is invaluable in punishment, compared to other tying ups. There's a variation where one adds heavy leg irons for a better restriction; the Sub is compelled to move at a really slow pace and it can therefore be very helpful for stillness, posture and a good training, ensuring that the Sub moves with grace and decorum.

Crab tie

The crab tie ties the Subs wrists to her/his ankles and usually adds ropes tying around the level of knees and elbows too, to keep her/his lower arms parallel to her/his lower legs. When perfectly and comfortably tied it is excitingly restrictive, allowing only the opening and closing of Subs legs and rolling onto her/his back. The Sub may try a semi-standing position which is really not that stable and therefore not recommended.

Bent Over The Chair

When one has furniture to rely on, it becomes even more interesting since imagination becomes wider as well as possibilities. Just use whatever makes it comfortable to tie wherever and enjoy your fun.

Waitress

This position refers to any given pose where the elbows are restrained behind the back but the wrists are constrained in front. A bar can be used to achieve the effect too. The name was given since the Sub can bring drinks but can't much benefit from it, only to please the guests or in your case, the guest.

Over The Pit Of Doom ("The Offering")

This basic tie has become mainstream due to many Hollywood damsel-in-distress scenes. It's really easy, the wrists are tied together and bound up above the head, while the ankles are kept strongly distant from each other with the use of a spreader bar. The primary goal and effect is one of great vulnerability, the Sub is unable to protect her/his modesty or better yet his/hers more sensitive areas from punishment.

The same goes with all positions where hands are raised above the head, this position shouldn't be maintained for too long since it can lead to circulation problems and the possibility of fainting. The broad band of rope or, better yet padded suspension cuffs, are recommended for use in order to avoid excessive pressure. This should only be used really briefly and only with cuffs.

As previously said, some positions are as simple, and/or as effective in reminding the Sub of its position within the privacy of your home, meaning true authority of a Dom.

There's a variation with legs tied together and it's usually referred to as Virgin Over The Pit Of Doom; with the spreader bar it can be referred to as Slut Over The Pit Of Doom but this choice of words is not the preferred. 'Slut' normally refers to a position where the Sub holds their legs wide open, rather than having them forced apart. So generally it should be assumed a spreader bar when referring the position, unless it is qualified by 'virgin' or 'modest'.

Caterpillar

Any kind of rope which goes the full length of the body is referred to as caterpillar or a rope cocoon. In many cases, a rope web with the similarity in construction to the karada goes the full length of the body, starting at the ankles and finishing at the Subs shoulders.

It has no use or function but a decorative one, even though the leg binding is actually effective, it does not provide any special security of a typical cinched tie like the Classic Damsel.

The ropes have their tendency to slip as the Sub moves. This can be a bit modified by front-back cinches or additional horizontal rope bands, but then it looses the decorative purpose of karada style. A more tougher alternative is to compose multiple rope bands, each cinched, making a variation that one of ways of rope mummification.

The absolute variation is full mummification, where bandages - saran wrap or tape are used to strongly enclose the Sub from head to toe. When diving into this variation, keep in mind the possible wrong outcomes and be prepared accordingly. Since one can overheat, you'll have to have safety scissors immediately available.

Bottoms Up

This one is absolutely a show off for putting one's sensitive's on display, and is famous for ways of restraining and feet punishment. The use of the crotch harness secured to the ceiling provides a Dom a great place for show off. This position allows even sexual access and a less decorative simple paired rope can be used even for the crotch section.

Many recommend it. Yes, bondage benches are mostly crafted to keep the Sub right in this position (normally with the use of leather straps to tie down wrists and ankles, and/or with a broad strap around the waist). This position is famous by having a whipping bench (or fucking bench) and sometimes the position itself is named after this feature.

Olympic Mascot

In the honor of the London 2012 Olympic Games, this position for a Sub was named 'Olympic Mascot'. Even though it's about touching the toes in an unbound position, Olympic Mascot also has a chain version of the crotch rope sit harness. This doesn't allow the Sub to take some of her/his weight on the chain, therefore the Sub has to go on the tiptoes position.

It combines the look of 'starters orders' and 'touching toes' with an awesome strong metalwork, and it's said to be much more Olympian in spirit than the original official Olyimpic symbol.

Box-Tie Variant

This is one of the most useful of all bondage positions, compared to those written before this one. This is purely a variation to the theme. For example, the plain rope bands at the front of the Sub have been decorated and spread with nice over-the-shoulder passes and tensioned rope twists to make a tie that retains all the best features of the basic box-tie whilst using more imagination.

The box tie can be referred to as the Ushiro Takatekote ("behind the back bound hands and arms"); we more commonly use the 'box tie' name since it's easier to pronounce.

Box-tie Balltie

And another variant on the box-tie is used as the basis of a balltie. As it has been said before, you must be careful with rope bondage near the neck. Anchor the rope which produces the balltie by running it over the shoulders either side of the neck and down to the box-tie, and there it can be secured, rather than going with it directly around the back of the neck.

Ebi ('Prawn')

This is just a more hardcore version of the tie above, where the rope pulling the Sub over is much shorter and logically the fold produced in her/his body much more emphasized. Once again, please be aware that the rope is secured to the box-tie to prevent any kind of pressure on the neck. Also, this should be used only for a short period of time, since originally this was used for real-life torture and when tied tightly and left for a longer duration than 5-10 minutes, can cause damages to the Sub.

Simple Egyptian

There are few examples of how the same basic position may be used and incorporated into ties of really different styles. The arm position is all about the straight-forward hands-crossed-in-front position which is referred to as the 'Egyptian'. Usually, a bit of rope is used. Contrary to the belief that it's not restraining as it seems, the tie is quite strong and secured.

Adding a rope around one ankle tied to a post or ring in the dungeon gives a final touch to the position. The other leg is normally tied in a frog-tie.

Crossed Arm Geisha

In this bondage position the Sub is forced with ropes into the same Egyptian pose so even though the Subs hands are not really restrained, she/he is able to maintain the integrity of the pose itself. All of these ropes are twisted into a nicely done, minimalistic crotch and hip harness. This design specifically is really popular due to its lifting and shaping effect on the ass cheeks of the Sub, and is well known for its pressure points on some extremely intimate locations.

Egyptian Spider's Web

This is one variation of bondage that goes above and beyond imagination and decoration. Once again the Sub has to be in a usual Egyptian posture, but now the ropes are laid over in a way to as to almost provide a target shield in front of her/him. The spider's web pattern is to be used to secure her/him in a cross-legged position too.

Pork Roll and Rope Ladder

Here the arms are tied in box-tie as before. However, keep in mind the two different forms of binding can be used on the limbs. The bent leg is wrapped in rope in a way which looks like a 'pork roll' method of binding a limb. Please do ignore all the bad connotations and be aware that the term is only for descriptive purposes.

The extended leg is tied in another style mastered by the Japanese, which is referred to as a 'rope ladder'. The rope is wrapped against itself many times as it ladders its way up the limb, a technique which is best used with natural fibres (like hemp) and is frequently used in the Japanese tradition too. Be aware that when you use slippery artificial ropes such as nylon, you're basically doomed.

A rope is used directly behind the neck to the extended leg, which should be treated with caution as discussed many times previously.

The asymmetric result, especially when the rope ladder is extended to a suspension point above, is commonly seen in the Japanese style rather than in the West (that is more symmetrical). So easily described, this would go something like: Lying on side, arms in box. One leg bent, in pork roll, the other extended upwards to ceiling, tied in a rope ladder, with rope from bottom of rope ladder on leg behind back to fold her over.

Teppo

The classic Japanese position, which it can be tied in several ways. The first example is tying the arms up to the ceiling, leaving the legs free to move. Even though giving the Sub the ability to move, this position is supposed to portray helplessness, since the ceiling rope prevents moving more than 3 feet or so.

The second variation also uses ropes up to the ceiling, but this time it's a sitting version with a rope web around the foot elevating one leg, and a rope gag being made into the teppo.

Japanese Reverse Prayer

The tie shows one way in which a Sub can be bound into the reverse prayer position incorporating ropes, which restrains Sub's fingers. The bondage is finished off by two rope wraps, which make the Sub stay in a kneeling position, which is anchored by a single rope slipper on one foot.

Asymmetry in Japanese-inspired positions is once again seen here; if you're more of a symmetrical Western style type, then you would choose to mirror that rope work on the other foot, even though it can be functionally too much. Actually, the use of rope slippers is not usually encouraged for Restrained Elegance Subs, since there are risks of the rope distorting the shape of the foot.

Lotus with Rope Ladder Gauntlet

For this position, the leg tie depends upon the ability of the Sub to attain the position, either full or half lotus, and hold it without the help of the rope for some period of time in order for the tie to be nicely and neatly applied. As long as the Sub can remain in and maintain the position in normal comfort without the presence of a rope, she/he ought to be able to do so while being bound.

The arms are bound together along with the forearms, using the rope ladder style, to form a rope gauntlet.

Bunny Ears / Futomomo Delta

The name applied for this position is two-fold. First we handle the arms, that are bound bent and raised, wrists crossed behind the Subs neck. Due to the silhouette that's made, comes the first name – bunny ears.

The legs are bound with the same style which reminds you of the classical Japanese form known as Futomomo; the addition of the rope around the opposite ankle pulling that same ankle to the Subs opposite ankle. Wrapped, the thigh forms a triangular shape which one can label with the Greek nomenclature of 'delta'.

Hammerlock

The position (and its variations) were introduced to the Restrained Elegance repertoire by Temptress Kate originally. The position gets its name from an arm lock used to restrain suspects by the police.

In the first version of the hammerlock tie, the hands are balled into fists. In this version, the fingers are incorporated into a tie, being one of the basic foundations that make the addition of ropes crossing the shoulders to keep the hands in raised position not relevant to this variant.

An addition of a single rope slipper converts the position into a simplified balltie. Moreover, the position can be intensified by adding nipple clamps, against which the Sub will be absolutely powerless.

Crossbow

This is a variation on the basic hogtie theme, exchanging a rope from the ankles to one around the upper body following the basic layout of the box tie for the rope between wrists and ankles normally used to get a similar posture in the Western hogtie.

It has all the advantages of the Western forms of helplessness. It lends to tying cross-legged, which some Subs find easier than the legs-together variations. It is also a lot more difficult to stand than the elbows-together variant tied with straight arms.

Koala Pole

This variation of this tie is used on a free-standing rattan pole. A more restraining and restrictive variation would be using a fixed pole. Use your imagination accordingly!

Diving Springboard

This position is a part of the trilogy of lookalikes of wrists-bound-to-legs in front poses, with the wrists bound to the ankles. (Legs up, wrists to knees shows them tied to the knees and the legs-up balltie but it also includes wrists to ankles, but with the rope running across the limbs bound rather than ankles together, wrists together and a joining rope). When the legs are raised, this can form a rather challenging tie.

As with all raised positions, you have to be responsible and be wary of a lack of circulation in the raised extremities of your Sub.

Bent Over Kneeling

This position is one of the basic ones of combinations of legs bound to keep the Sub on his/her knees, arms bound behind (usually with a single rope at the wrists) and a rope raising the arms to produce the binding. It is great for convincing a bad Sub to properly honour her Dom, with their mouth being placed at a very reasonable height for the purpose. The effectiveness and restraint can depend on the elevation of the bondage.

One of the variants binds the legs together and keeps them bent; if you want a Sub to have a better range of movement – the right way to do so would be to tie the legs in a frog-tie.

As with all bondages, everything depends on the very shape and flexibility of the Sub; those with narrow shoulders and long arms will find it really easy, while those with broader or more muscular shoulders and short arms can be unable to do the position at all. You must reason with yourself before doing this position and be aware of your possibilities at all times.

Front-Back Box Tie

If you read every possibility carefully, you'll recognize this 'wraparound' concept, where two pairs of handcuffs were used to attach the wrists to the upper arm (just above the elbow) of the opposite arms. This time we tie it with rope. The box tie is a foundation, but with one arm in front and the other behind. The box tie rule (that the hands cannot be moved out of the agreed position because of the ropes around the upper arms) is used, but is backed up by the vertical ropes over the shoulders and crotch-rope, which are bound into the box tie to secure the whole creation.

Note that good research for further possibilities of this bound is needed in this area and be careful when trying out things.

Bent Over Bamboo Spreader

This is a position where the legs are spread wide, and the hands placed in between those legs in a position where there's a lot imagination involved and therefore varies by person how this can be used and bounded.

Yoko Tzury

Yoko Tzury (or Zuri or Tsuri) is a sideways suspension, and the name could be easily called a Peter Pan sideways suspension too. This semi-suspension has the same basic characteristic of a sideways extension (the leg) held up by the ropes.

Hishi Fit

The basis of this particular tie is the harness tied around the waist and upper thighs, which is called a 'sit harness'. The use is the same – the bulk of the weight is used by the thigh loops, with the waist element giving security and distribution of weight to the waist and/or hips in some ways. It provides a comfortable and safe support capable of taking the Sub's weight for a really long period of time.

A Brief Heads Up On Suspensions

Any tie that involves the whole of the Sub's weight being taken on the ropes is serious and dangerous (increased risk of nerve damage from box-ties taking weight on upper arms when it's not tied correctly). Every increase in height rising from the ground is a greater danger as well as responsibility. You have to be ready at all times if anything goes wrong, like during an inverted suspension where the hands are unable to protect the head, and please start practicing these more complicated techniques only when you have practiced the easier ones for a long period of time, so you're fully aware of the risks that they carry.

Please don't play with even the simplest suspensions if you're not ready for that kind of responsibility, care, and attention. Always make sure the suspension is secure and that everything is done properly and according to plan. Test all your tools and ropes beforehand. Before getting into anything, please educate yourself, read about possible risks and how something should be done concerning the tools, space where suspension should be done and the person you're about to restrain.

Basic Horizontal Suspension

This is one of the easiest suspensions to do. The basic idea is that the weight is taken by multiple broad bands of rope, especially under the arms, at the waist, at the hips, under the bum and above the knees. (The ankle and wrist ropes are not particularly weight bearing). The rope bands are always secured in place by additional ropes to prevent slippage – this would prevent the ropes sliding off if Sub were to start going back and forth.

This 'rope hammock' position is one of the more comfortable ones out there, and it allows the tie to be done while on the floor and then the Sub is pulled up gradually, while testing the weight distribution as the Sub struggles all around. It's always the same with suspensions, you have to adjust the tension of some of the ropes going up to the suspension bar to get the wanted look and distribution of weight between the different rope bands. You can use much broader bands for the 'stay' ropes over the shoulders.

Peter Pan Sideways Suspension

This is a Japanese style suspension using fewer turns of rope, very carefully positioned. This one isn't the one that should be done at home, especially if you're new to this. Here it's written only for education purposes, if you want to see it and maybe even try it, please contact someone who does it professionally.

Inverted Single Leg Suspension

This really is a terrifying type of inverted suspension- it's hard to even look at let alone do it! The duration of a person hanging is a couple of minutes, which gives you a sense of how dangerous this suspension is. If you do somehow get the courage to try this out, please take care of your partner, and if you're the one who's up there, please say something before it becomes urgent!

Chapter 8. Punishment and All the How-To's

There are many ways to enjoy BDSM and they vary from person to person. So, let's explore some of these ways.

The great help of toys

Clothespins are great toys. They can be clamped to all kinds of body parts, and the sensation is out of this world, especially when it's on sensitive parts of the body, such as nipples. Moreover, the longer the clothespins are on the body part, the greater the sensation when they're removed. They can be clamped to nipples or just breasts in general; on the sides of arms, legs, and thighs or any other place that arouses you.

Note that the plastic clothespins create more intense arousal than wooden ones, and small clothespins are sharper than the larger ones.

Make a zip strip: If you are an adventurous type, use six wooden clothespins and make a small hole in one handle of each one them, near the end. Afterward, tie the clothespins along a piece of twine, leaving four inches or so between the clothespins. The result is a "zipper" or "zip strip," it's a series of clothespins that can be clamped in a row on your partner's body.

A pair of chopsticks and a few rubber bands can be used to make something like clamps. Put the chopsticks above and below the nipples, or along each slide of the clitoris, and rubber-band them together at the ends.

Spanking toys are available from all kinds of sources and you can also go totally DIY. Wooden spoons, paint stirrers, and rubber or plastic ice scrapers that you use to clear ice from a windshield is great for making paddles for spanking.

Snake bite kits

These are available everywhere where you can get camping supplies and department stores, and they include suction cups that provide a great amount of suction, and therefore a great amount of arousal. These work like a charm on nipples, and on the clitoris too.

Ordinary dental floss makes nice nipple bondage. Tie a slipknot of a piece of dental floss and pull it snug on the Sub's nipples.

Remote-controlled vibrators and butt plugs can be found at all sex stores. They're fun to play with alone, but in a group or semi-public settings they are a true party starter. You can, for example, equip the submissive person with a remote-controlled toy of some sort, and then go out to dinner with friends.

Brushes of various sorts are excellent for bare skin, it gets better if the Sub is blindfolded. For example, many start with a make up one then go to the hair or paint brush then finish with electric toothbrush which is a true game changer. All of these are for external use, of course.

A bamboo skewer – the one used in the kitchen is really an interesting toy when it's used on a Sub that's restrained and blindfolded. You have to play slowly and leaving a certain pressure on the skin, then it feels much sharper than it normally is. When used on sensitive areas like breasts, the sensation gives out the feeling of really piercing the skin with a needle, even though the skewer won't break the skin.

Ice is great for all-purpose sex and is a frequent sex toy that's available to everyone. You can always go old school and just put some ice down the partner's body, or just spice it up a bit with putting it in your mouth and then go down on your partner.

A more interesting variation is to make an ice dildo, of course if you have that amount of time to spare. In order to do this, you'll need a plain unlubricated condom and the cardboard tube from the centre of the roll of paper towels. Cut the cardboard tube lengthwise, then close it into a cylinder that's as wide as you want the dildo to be, and tape it. Fill the condom with water, tie it in order to shut it, and suspend it in the tube with a piece of string; the cardboard tube will prevent the bulging of water in the dildo.

Place it upright in the freezer. A few hours later, you'll have a new-age dildo made of ice and in whatever the size you like! You can use it for vaginal or anal play. Please play smart, before penetration run some water over your body parts to prevent the ice from sticking to your privates.

Bubble wrap can be used to make an unusual dildo in any width you want. Take a length of bubble wrap and roll it tightly, bubble-side out for better texture and pleasure, until it's as thick enough. Place a condom over the already made roll of bubble wrap, and put a rubber band or tape at the end of the condom in order for it to stay in one place.

Dice and cards can also be kinky in all kinds of interesting variations for your sex life. You can make 3x5" index cards with questionable pictures of your partner and/or you, or you can just buy them in a shop and just play away.

A punishment box is a great thing when you're a Dom that wants his Sub to be properly taught. It's connected to the cards, as mentioned above, you can make every one of them with a punishment written on it. When the Sub doesn't follow the general rules, the Dom can make the Sub draw their card from the box. Or, if preferred, make your Sub do the job of picking the cards while they're aroused.

Of course, while making your punishment box you have to think of the partner's needs and wishes since something might arouse you but it can disgust your partner, so make your cards accordingly. Some of the ideas might be:

- The Sub is not allowed to orgasm alone or generally for the next two days.

- The Sub will be spanked.

- The Sub has to wear clothespins on his/her nipples for half an hour.

- The Sub will be denied an orgasm but will be brought right to it.

And so on, and so on. It can be even kinkier or something less than this, whatever works for you is fine. If you're a bit creative, you can make a game out of making a punishment cards. Like, if one of the proposals for the cards isn't fine by one of the two of you, the one who proposed it gets to be punished. Meta-punishments can be fun, too. One punishment card might be to draw two cards and must be punished by the orders of both or to flip a coin and determine which side means one card draw and which two.

A Path to Adventure: You both write questions that can be answered with simple yes/no answers then make your partner answer the questions. Questions should vary by your needs and wishes, but can be written in a matter like: Will I be spanked? Will you be tied?

Marble bag: You both make a punishment box (which is filled with cards describing things the submissive doesn't like to do) and a reward box (which is filled with cards with things the submissive does like), and then fill a bag with twenty marbles, ten black and ten white or you can use whatever is easier for you just to distinguish these two. This can be used against a Sub if the Sub isn't obedient enough, Dom takes a white marble from the bag and replaces it with the black one ruining the chance of a Sub. Though, the vice versa can be done too, so increasing the Subs chances for having a nice treatment.

Points for Freedom: The whole idea of this is that the Sub does everything the Dom instructs until he/she can get her/his freedom. The Sub earns freedom by winning "points." To earn them, the Sub agrees to do certain things, which are something like punishments and a punishment box can be used for this game too, though it has to be modified. Each activity has to have a certain number of points that go with it that varies depending on how difficult or uncomfortable the activity is. The Sub is free to choose from the activities to earn points any time he/she likes, but otherwise is a complete slave until reaching a count of 100 points whether it takes days or months to achieve it.

Same with the game of rewards and punishments, the activities and their point value will vary depending on what you agree on. Here are some of the ideas you can use or just to light up your own imagination:

- The Sub has to masturbate right until the very orgasm for the Doms entertainment. The first, second, third, and fourth orgasm are worth nothing while each orgasm after that earns one point (or more, whatever pleases you).

- If the Sub does not shave his/her pubic hair, the Sub has to shave it completely for a total of 5 points.

Knives can be fun when used properly, and are psychologically proven sex toys. No, you don't cut your partner for pleasure. A semi-sharp or pointed knife edge just drawing over skin, but not hard enough to cut the skin, is really intense and a sensation that gets the partner in a state of craze – definitively when done with blindfolds. When the knife is in a freezer right before the use, then it feels even sharper than it really is. If you're using it on a blindfolded person, they might actually think you're cutting their skin open. Avoid extra sensitive skin and play on backs, legs and thighs for great pleasure.

Saran wrap as a great erotic tool. As mentioned before, bondage doesn't always involve ropes and chains. Plain saran wrap works okay for bondage. Your partner should be sitting or lying on their side while they wait to be bound in a cocoon of the saran wrap. It's highly secure, and a nude person wrapped in see-through wrap is quite sexy. The saran wrap allows all sorts of interesting play, from play with ice cubes to more intense with knife tips. Spanking, poking, pinching, and anything else that makes it doable while the partner is bound is okay, but please avoid doing all of this with a blindfold. Also, please remember that saran wrap can make a person overheat, so take care of your partner by using a fan or just instantly removing the wrap but have some clothing for the aftershock of cooling down so they can get their temperature back on track.

Vet wrap is another great way to bound your partner. Vet wrap has the same fabric material as Ace bandages, but is less expensive and available for buying in much longer rolls and different colors. You can find it online or any pet store, and when used can quite effectively immobilize the person. A fun variation of mummification with saran wrap or vet wrap is to arouse them while they're mummified, playing with their body parts and seeing how they respond. You can penetrate the Sub with vibrators or butt plugs, put on clamps or you can use remote controlled vibrator.

Bungee cords are really interesting bondage gear. It's something that's easily found in a hardware store for securing loads in a car, but is also excellent for bounding someone. Pad or cover the place where the hooks meet the cord, and latch the cords around the bed. Bungee cords are deceptive; a person bound this way might feel like they can escape or slip, but they're really safe.

Techniques

Realism in scenarios

Many scenarios involve someone being taken by "force". The clothes being torn apart and the whole thing seems great to try out, but first make sure you buy some clothes to be torn apart in a thrift shop.

Extended Penetration

It's possible to, with certain practice, to train someone for vaginal and/ or anal penetration for extended periods of time. Porn stars use it all the time, so you can try it out too, with caution of course. So, it's possible for a person to walk around with a butt plug or a dildo throughout the day. Sure, you have to start small and it might be painful, and no one can make you do it no matter who they are. When the pain is unbearable just stop!

Sensory Deprivation

Tactile senses are everything. Have you ever thought about how much others are enhanced when some are taken away? Tie your partner, blindfold them and put in earplugs that you can find in any drug store. All of this makes an experience more intense. There are also special hoods called "ball hoods" that work really well and cover ears and eyes but are psychologically really intimidating, and besides all that they're quite expensive.

You can even use headphones/earphones and play some static music if it's okay with your partner and it will work the same.

Human Sex Doll

This is a dream come true for those who don't lack creativity. The rules are simple: the Subs partner is a living sex toy, and allows the Dom to put him or her into any given position and take any kind of action, and the Sub must remain completely passive throughout the whole thing. The Sub simply has to remain in whatever position the Dom places him or her into, and can't take any active role in any way whatsoever as the Dom explores the Subs body.

One variation of this is the idea that involves tying the Sub toughly in a sexually picked out position, and then exploring the Subs body in a humiliating and/or uncomfortable way and all that while having sex with the Sub. During this whole time the Sub is forbidden to make any movement or sound or respond in any way. If the Sub disobeys, punishment is in order.

Enforced Availability

A specific time of day must be picked for a sex, no matter the arousal of the partners. Throughout the day, if the Sub is available to Doms, Dom can take care of a Sub in any way possible for sex or just sexual arousal. It's a Subs job to get aroused and take care of lubrication. Please keep in mind this has to be arranged and the consent must be given beforehand.

Eroticising everyday activities

There are various ways to implement it in everyday lives, you just have to keep an open mind. You can go to a pet store and try out collars and buy the nicest one, or just buy some things in a supermarket that have usually a sexual context like bananas, cucumber, condoms and so on. This creates a simple pleasure out of buying simples things and there's a psychological effect where the Sub thinks that everybody is aware what's going on.

Public play

This isn't a game for everyone since it makes a Sub feel vulnerable in more ways than one. But here are some suggestions like, buy your partner extremely sexy lingerie and make them go to the office in it, which is a constant reminder that they're a Sub in the relationship.

Or if you're more hardcore, you can rope a harness that can be made with thin twine or cord. Tie the harness around your partner's torso, and then have your partner wear the harness beneath his or her clothing. As the Sub moves, the harness moves all around against his or her body, and works as a reminder for the Sub that it's there.

Some even think of a sex toy while dining in a restaurant and give it out to their Sub to masturbate with it and/or to come out of the bathroom with the toy inside them. Please be careful while playing and picking out the toys to play with.

The Sealed List

This is great for long-distance relationships, or if someone just travels much and isn't around. Make a list of things your Sub can do and put in an envelope. Mark the envelopes and make sure you write on every list of paper when the Sub can open the next one. The rule is, you can't open all at once and each envelope must give instructions for what has to be done to arouse the Sub.

Conditioning Vol.1

Thanks to the human brain, which continues to learn in so many different ways and learns how to function constantly, everything can be used for kinky things. One of the ways to condition your partner is for them to want something they usually wouldn't and test their limits. You have to pick something that's hard, within their limits, and what they would never normally ask for. It has to be something you'd use as a punishment and something that would be really humiliating for them.

You have to explain this action to your partner in every single detail, with such passion that it gives them a sense of security while they're still cringing at the very thought of it. You have to be precise and actually sell it to them and at the very end tell them you won't do it. It's purely psychological, they'll start asking questions and even beg for it but let them work for it until you give out. They're not even aware of what you've done and keep it that way until the last moment.

It becomes logical to them, when they start begging they start actually wanting it, even though it isn't something they're prone to or something they had wanted to do.

Conditioning Vol.2

Another fun thing to do is actually training your partner. It might sound silly, but try it and it won't sound that silly anymore. Whenever your partner starts cumming, continue saying one word in particular. Next time do it right before they cum and the next time start right before they cum and until the very end of it. Do so for a longer period of time and then suddenly just say the word in unconventional settings and watch them wiggle out of embarrassment.

Conditioning Vol.3

Find an object or jewellery that your partner will wear only when they're aroused. Then first, arouse the Sub by any means possible. When they're on top of their arousal put the ring on or whatever object you picked out and remove it when the arousal starts to fade. As the time goes by, the ring itself will become associated with the arousal. When you get to that point it will be easy for a Sub just to get aroused by putting on the ring.

Conditioning Vol.4

Get a bell or chime which the Sub will wear during sex. After some period of time they'll associate it with the sex itself and will get aroused just by the sound of it. If the Sub is okay with it, you can actually try it out in public for a new kind of high.

Dirty Talking/Dirty Writing

Many enjoy this and it can be done in many ways, like saying dirty nicknames or just about what you want to do to your partner and how. Some talks about fantasies are also considered as dirty talk, and even though you think you're not proficient yet you might start liking it by practicing it. It may at first feel weird and funny but you'll get past it.

Sexting is mainstream and there's a reason why. It deletes the face to face interaction and makes it even easier to lay loose. You can write about fantasies, scenarios or whatever is more of a thing between your partner and you.

Write on the Subs body

Talking dirty is great fun, drawings are even more fun but putting all of that on your partner is the best of all. You can write dirty words, nicknames or just what you want to do to your partner. This is fun because it can be done in public by ordering your Sub to go to the bathroom and write on whatever part of body some word or anything, masturbate and come back without anyone else knowing except the two of you. It can be done even as a public play like marking your territory on their chest or wherever and them going with that to work, of course with clothes that cover it.

Long-Distance Relationships

This shouldn't stop lovers from being sexually active. But in today's world that's running on technology, you can always have cybersex, video chat, phone sex and what not.

The public setting can be used even for long-distance relationships, since they can call their partners while they're in a restaurant or a bar and order them what to do in a bathroom. Since all phones come with a camera, you might even use it so you can all enjoy the orders.

Chapter 9. Live up to Your Role Play

Sexual desire is very diverse since it is personal, and sometimes we feel ashamed to share it with anyone else. There are a variety of methods to overcome your inhibitions and every minute couples are getting started with their own role play. Sexual role play is not something that was just created, the idea of role play goes way back to ages when they weren't even aware of it yet.

The possibilities of role play are solely limited only the imagination of a person, so if you're up for a challenge or just something to get you fired up, here it goes:

Surprise Beginnings

This is a great way to start your evening. Get a bag and fill it with whatever you want to use during sex, so it can be cuffs, sexy outfits or whatnot. Place it next to the door or wherever you want, but make sure you write directions properly so the Sub knows they can't enter your bedroom without stripping down and getting into whatever you left in that bag.

Naughty boarding school student

It's just a variation of the classic naughty Catholic schoolgirl, but this one features a boarding school student who has done something wrong and the headmistress must punish him accordingly. Whatever your imagination pleases can be used as an arousal for getting your partner in crime hard. Don't limit yourself to only soft tissues but explore their genitals during the foreplay.

Pony play

This game play is mostly focused on exploring one's body while the Sub plays the pony. The Dom tests all features of the pony since he/she's interested in buying and wants to know possible anomalies. Therefore, checks out teeth, muscles, genitals, how the pony moves, gallops and so on until the final goal – the ride of the pony. The crops can be used for some motivation for a pony like spanking and maybe some rope and a gag. And of course, some space.

The kinkier ones add a 'pony tail' (a fall of hair attached to a butt plug) which may be fun to comb but if the Sub's not up for it and is in pain it has to be removed instantly.

Ghost

This scenario is a role-play for three people, all must be lovers. One of them is a "ghost". The other two people have a hot-n-heavy make-out session in their bedroom, while the ghost does whatever he or she pleases to those two people. Those two cannot see or hear the ghost, but they can feel what he does, so they blame the other for the things he/she's done.

Interrogation

This role play needs two people from which one has some information the other one needs. If you can't come up with something, you can just pick a card and the other one has to make you say it which is it. The scene can start with that dominant capturing what we've seen on shows and restraining the person who's going to be interrogated and/ or strip them down for a check. They can be tied to a chair and can go through classic BDSM torture if that's part of the game. So clothespins, spanking, paddling and so on is ON.

Naturally the session intensifies as the interrogated person declines to cooperate and when he/she finally gives out the information the sex starts.

Night Security

One plays someone who's trespassing and the other is the guard. Usually the guard is the Dom and the Sub is the other. The guard confronts the offender and gets him to the questioning room where the strip search happens. The Guard tells the offender that police have to be notified about this but some other arrangements can be made if they follow instructions. Since all this in normal conditions has to be videotaped, the guard can videotape those arrangements and agreements that he and the offender have made and keep them to himself.

The Prize

In this scenario the Sub is a stripper that works in an "anything goes" night club and there is a prize for the best dance. The winner gets the prize, and the prize is the stripper to whom he can do whatever he pleases without any rules attached.

Secret past

In this scenario the Sub has some dark, secret past he/she's ashamed of and doesn't want anyone else to know about it. One night someone knocks on the door, threatening to expose the Sub to the world. That's when the Sub makes a pact with the devil and gives out sexual favours for his/hers silence. From that point on, the blackmailer can do whatever he wants with the Sub.

The Hostage

This scenario is best when well played out, so you might want to sit down and invest in it. Like arranging a motel room on the edge of the town, and the kidnapping of the innocent and nice victim. You're the notorious criminal and the victim stands no chance against you. You can play out the mock-rape at the end or just become two lovebirds that realized their love for each other in a very different way.

The Photo Shoot

This one is great since you get to have something to remember it by. One acts as a professional photographer, mastering nudity as a form of creation and the other is a client who just wants a personal set of photos for a special part of the house. The session starts, you get a few great photos. After the shoot is over, the photographer wants his muse only for himself and that to be considered as a way of payment. The photographer may use the camera to take pictures during the payment too.

This can be used then as a scenario that was previously described, the "Secret past".

The Pirate

This one is basic and old, but frequently used. The Pirate gets into a village and takes one girl with him, rips her clothes of and while tightly having her pinned on the wall he tells her what he's going to do to her. Get into the role play by getting the outfit for the scenes.

Dinner and a Movie

Pure power exchange. Before going for a dinner or a move, decide who's Dom and who's Sub. The Dom creates the rules, like the Sub can't talk to anyone else beside the Dom or the Dom can only speak to the Sub and through the Sub with others. Dom gives out rules and the Sub follows, same goes if the Sub is ordered to go to the bathroom and to strip down or just to get teased in a darkened theatre.

The key of the role play is that no one else can know the trick and you both have to stay in a character.

Mad Scientist

One plays the mad scientist, obviously, and the other is the victim of his experiment. The scientist can do whatever he pleases and however he pleases. This game can be done in polyamorous relationships, so a three way is an option, just add a lab assistant and voila!

Ravishment

It starts with a nice evening at home doing whatever you think is appropriate. Then, after a serious make out session the Sub refuses to go further and the other pushes him to do so. When the Dom gets the arousal of Sub declining to participate, the Sub gets tied up by the Dom and the Sub continues to beg for freedom.

Crime and Punishment

Make some idiotic rule which the other will break, in that matter you're the cop in that situation. Arrest the offender of the law and use your handcuffs, tie them up to a chair or on a bed. If the offender is too loud, he/she can always get gagged. Depending on your kinks, you can go for a trial and get sentenced for spanking or bounding. Maybe some bribe can be in order, who knows.

Switch Tease

The girl captures a guy and blindfolds him. Then she changes her clothes before him, and on that very sound he gets aroused. She takes off his blindfold and starts to tease him. He somehow sets himself free and ties her up and you know what goes after that...

Exchange of Power

(More for bondage fans, rather than D/S fans)

She dresses up – black lace bustier, gloves, stockings and high heeled boots; so full Dom apparel. Her weapon of choice is a whip, and she continues to tease him and harass him in her own way. At one point he goes crazy, sets himself free, knocks her out and chooses if he'll go full on romance and lean for a long kiss or he'll play tough and get her back for all those whip swings.

Playing Army

This can be done two ways: The resistance fighter has been captured by the local garrison and tied to a chair, interrogated in order for them to find out the location of the secret base; or the soldier has been caught by the guerrillas, who will be more than willing to provide ruthless treatment. Have fun picking sides and costumes and seeing how everything plays out.

Burglar

This is mostly played out as a man playing a burglar who tells his friend or a partner how some burglar seeks out for women with *put specifics of our partner* and then add some information like if she's home during a specific time or likes to walk around in lingerie. Tell her how they tend to watch and then break in, not that that will be a problem since she leaves the door open.

So, literally, you're giving her a game plan for how she has to dress and where to be at what time for you to come in and act out your burglar character. After the act of the burglar, you get to be her boyfriend that comes to the rescue.

Burglar Vol.2

This time, the burglar just goes in and starts making a mess and gets caught. Offers anything in exchange for the silence so the police don't know about this.

Exorcism

This one is really complex, and one has to act to be possessed by the demon and the other is the exorcist.

The demon isn't willing to go and gets to seduce the exorcist out. In this scenario you get to have very kinky humiliation play filled with dirty words and actions.

The Deprogramming

This scenario is also complex and it's about a victim of a cult and unethical deprogrammer. He's trying to undo everything the cult has done to the victim, but the victim loses her way and can't tell right from wrong. The deprogrammer takes advantage of that and makes the victim do whatever he pleases, and afterward erases it from her memory.

Chapter 10. BDSM Vocabulary

You may have read many, if not even all of these before, but you probably haven't got the real sense of some of them and their true meaning. Let's go one final time over some things that were mentioned, and some that couldn't be incorporated to the newbies life of BDSM.

24/7 – It's all about a power exchange relationship (that can and almost always includes big and/or small aspects of life) and it goes on all day, every day.

Aftercare – It's a period of time after session when players (partners) check in and re-establish connections with one another. It usually includes cuddling, sex, eating or drinking, all while talking about the scene / session and/ or checking in. Aftercare varies for everyone, and can also just be focused on some alone time, or whatever possible personal preferences. Aftercare is widely known to be a huge part of kinky play that's a definite must.

Ageplay – Roleplay involving a distinct difference in ages, and often power exchange based on those ages. Can include infantilism, parent/child play, incest play, daiper play, etc.

BDSM – A modern acronym used to refer to the kink and fetish communities and activities. Letters stand for many different things, including "Bondage and Discipline," "Dominance and Submission," "Sadomasochim," "Sadism and Masochism," and "Slave/Master."

Bondage – Restraint or restriction of a subject, often used to refer to a preference (i.e., "I like bondage"). It can include rope bondage, variations of suspension bondage, different kinds of leather bondage, even furniture and device bondage, and last but not least – predicament bondage. Bondage can have only to do with dominance, or just sex, as a way of art, or everything all together.

Bottom – A role referring to the person receiving sensation.

Breathplay – The act of choking and/or restricting breath. Breathplay is a topic of debate in many kink circles because of the difficulty of the risks involved; it is considered very dangerous, and falls into the category of edgepay.

CBT – Acronym for "Cock and Ball Torture," usually also including specific techniques and anatomical understanding for the torture of male genitalia.

Cane/Caning – A common BDSM toy and activity. Canes can be made from many different materials, including different woods, plastics, or any semi-flexible material. The act of caning involves striking someone with a cane, usually across broad, fleshy areas of the body (the butt, the backs of the thighs, etc). Caning is also popular across the bottoms of the feet.

Collar/Collaring – It can represent someone's identity as a submissive and/or owned person, a collar can be imbued with whatever meaning by the wearer, or none at all, although it often carries some symbolic weight. Collaring ceremonies are common in BDSM, and can range anywhere from a simple commitment or preference for wearing a collar, to a level of seriousness on-par with an engagement or marriage.

Consent – Saying yes! Saying yes please Sir or Madam! Consent is un-coerced, non-pressured, freely given permission. This is at the heart of all things kinky; consent is very, very important.

Consensual Nonconsent – Sometimes referred to as "rape play," ConNonCon includes much more than acting out violent fantasies. It is complex scene play, which usually has a pre-negotiated safeword and extensive discussion of boundaries and limits beforehand. During ConNonCon, the scene may have the outward appearance of being very violent, and without the consent of one party; essentially, a rape scene. Consensual Nonconsent, while it can be very hot, can also be serious mojo to play with; approach with caution. Try it with some soft bed restraints.

Corsetry/Tight-lacing – A fetish that explores power exchange and/or fetish through shape changing, sometimes breath-limiting corsetry.

Cupping – Also called "fire cupping," it is the act of heating up glass cups with rounded backs, usually a few inches across, on the skin. As the cups cool, they create a vacuum, leaving a hicky-like bruising pattern across the skin. If done hard enough/hot enough, cupping can also break the skin.

Dom(me) – A role identifying a person as dominant; to be on the controlling and decision-making side of power exchange (male: Dom, female: Domme). One who has, takes, or receives power. See also: submissive.

Dungeon – A word referring to large group play spaces or places where play parties are held. They are not real-life dungeons. Usually, they're just simple rooms converted into pleasure rooms, some even use ballrooms for conversion, or even their whole houses. A DIY made dungeon usually includes some kink furniture (things like spanking benches, crosses, suspension equipment, stocks, cages etc.), and they can serve as a common area to socialize and have drinks or whatever the needs, and a bit more private places that are meant for aftercare and cuddling. Dungeons by code have different kind of rules depending on whose is it.

Dungeon Master – A person responsible for safety in the Dungeon, usually an experienced member of the community, sometimes the host. They walk around, check in on different scenes, are responsible for ousting unsafe of inappropriate players etc.

D/S – Shorthand for Dominance and submission.

Edgeplay – It's a common term for BDSM uses that are considered at the edge, and can be more risky, and are frequently debated within the community. Some of the kinks that are used for edgeplay are: breathplay, choking, knifeplay, play peircing, bloodplay, fireplay, gun play, consensual nonconsent and many more since the imagination of one is endless

Enema – is the act of cleaning ones' anal cavity and his/her rectum. It can also be a fetish preference.

Fetish – A "fetish" is natural high that one gets from an object or action that can be but not exclusively sexual (for example: feet, leather, latex, choking, bounding), but whatever it is, it always carries sexual links or is an absolute turn-on for the individual person.

Fetlife – Kink's equivalent of facebook, fetlife.com is a website for posting pictures, statuses, writing, finding local groups, making friends, and organizing events.

Fire Play – Play that involves the sensation, use, or threat of fire. Considered edgeplay.

Fisting – A sexual act in which the giver's fist (or part thereof) is use to penetrate the receiving partner. When done with proper warm up and technique, fisting doesn't hurt or cause any damage, but rather can be really amazing! Fisting can be anal or vaginal.

Floggers/Flogging – A common BDSM toy and practice, a flogger is a multi-tailed whip. The tails can be made from various materials, such as leather, suede, or hair, often with wood or synthetic handles wrapped in the material of choice. Flogging can produce a sensation that's anywhere from a sharp sting to heavy thud, or any combination of the two. Hits from a flogger are best across a part of the body that's large and meaty, such as the upper thighs, butt, or upper back (but not) the lower back. Floggers come in many sizes, with any number of tails (and often specific names based on those numbers, such as a cat-o-nine-tails).

Golden Showers – the kink practice of peeing on someone and/or being peed on.

Hanky Code – Originally out of the gay leather scene, the hanky code uses different colors and materials of handkerchiefs (bandanas) to indicate areas of BDSM interest. Using the hanky code is often called "flagging," where at a bar or a party, a person would wear a certain color bandana in a certain pocket (right or left) to communicate preferences to others (example: black bandana in the left pocket indicates "into receiving/bottoming heavy SM).

Gorean – Based on the sci-fi novels by John Norman, Gorean households and couples follow a strict and traditional protocol, involving specific postures and rituals. Most Gorean relationships are 24/7 and Master/Slave.

Hard Limit – A specific element or action that a person isn't comfortable with, and cannot see themselves becoming comfortable with (example: "Golden showers are a hard limit for me").

Impact play - A category of sensation play, impact play is just what it sounds like, i.e., when something makes an impact. It can include but not be limited to, spanking, slapping, flogging, choking, punching, hitting, etc. and it refers to any possible activity where you hit or make a damage to someone with any object or just with your arms. The consequence is a production of two types of sensations – stings and thuds. A sting is a strike felt at the skin. It is mostly made by a thinner, harder, or lower mass material. A thud goes deeper into the muscle and is caused by a slower, heavier or softer object. Whipping and flogging can be very complicated and very technical, so they're not advised to do unless you have someone to show you the ropes of the job. The word whip is normally referred to a long, thin leather tail attached to a handle – visually similar to a bullwhip. When it is used properly it provides intense surface stinging, but it can also break the skin very easily.

Knife Play – As it says, it's a play that includes the use, threat, or sensation of playing with knives. Sometimes it's thought to be used as a part of an edgeplay.

Masochism/Masochist – Someone who enjoys pain/the act of enjoying pain. Can sometimes indicate the feeling of pain as pleasure, or the simple enjoyment of pain as pain.

Master/Slave – A relationship term indicating intense power exchange, service, and sometimes a 24/7 dynamic. A bit more specific and in variations different kind of D/S relationship, Master/slave can be sometimes thought of as a bit more extreme and/or more 24/7 oriented than a simple D/S.

Medical Play – play or scenes involving medical equipment, a medical aesthetic, and medical tools. Often involves needle play and/or play piercing.

Munch – A social event for kinksters, usually held at a bar or a restaurant (originates from the term "burger munch"), a munch doesn't involve play or sex, but rather an event for community to gather, talk, share interests, or plan events.

Mummification – the wrapping or mummifying of part of, or all of the body to confine movement and/or limit sensory experience. Can be done with saran wrap, plastic, rubber, fabric, or with special equipment like vaccubeds.

Needle Play – Play involving needles, or the threat of needles. See also: play piercing.

Play – A generally used verb to indicate doing BDSM actions, and an adjective to precede specific BDSM interests. Examples: "Needle play," "play piercing," "age play" and "play party."

Play Party – An event where kinksters gather to play. Play parties might be held in a dungeon or other kind of play space, or simply in someone's house. Play parties can differ by their size, rules, and even etiquette, but it often includes dressing up (or down), variations of many kink activities (bondage, sadomasochism, and sometimes sex). Most play parties involve public play, where within the context of the party, couples or groups will play in front of whoever else attends. See also: Dungeon, dungeon master.

Play Piercing – The practice of temporary piercing of the flesh, both for the sensation and aesthetic of piercing. Piercings are sometimes placed in designs across the body, or needles may be attached to string or other points for further sensation.

Pony Play – play involving acting like, or being the owner of, a human pony. It can involve a bit of costuming (something like hoof boots, saddles, bridals, bits), or just sounds and actions of the real-life horse. It almost always involves a way of power exchange between the two.

Power Exchange – The act of exchanging power, from one or more parties to one or more other parties, often in the form of control and/or sensation. Consent is at the basis of any healthy power exchange, regardless of whether the exchange lasts an hour, a day, or a lifetime.

Pet Play – it's a play that involves acting like, or being the owner of some animal, a human animal. Sometimes it includes costuming and proper props (like leashes, collars, food bowls), and it mostly involves some kind of power exchange.

RACK – "Risk Aware Consensual Kink," this acronym was born as a response to SSC, as a consent-culture and safety-oriented attitude that could include more inherently risky play in its scope.

Rape fantasy – When someone has fantasies and wishes of being raped; it can sometimes lead to some really complicated consent limits. It's sometimes referred to as a "rape play," but the term "consensual nonconsent," is more preferred since it explains the possibility of the role-playing rape being okay.

Rough Sex – even vanilla sex can get a bit rough, so it's a sex that includes anything rough: biting, scratching, power play, choking, spanking or whatever one thinks of rough.

Sadism/Sadist – A person that finds enjoyment in giving pain to another (usually their partner). Sadists enjoy pain for many different reasons depending on the personality; some are purely sexual, some are simply not

Safeword – a pre-negotiated word that either party (although most commonly the bottom) can use to pause, check-in, or end the scene or play. Safewords function in the same "no" or "stop" might otherwise (and part of their function is allowing the bottom to scream "no" or "stop" as much as they like). Some common safewords are "safeword," and the color system: "red" = stop, "yellow" = check in (some people also use various different colors to mean different things, for instance, "green" = please god don't stop, etc.).

Sensation Play – Play that involves the sense of touch, not necessarily pain. Playing with a flogger gently all across someone's skin for example can be thought as a sensation play.

Service Top – A specific kind of top, a service top usually describes their turn-on as how their actions are in service to the bottom (example: "I like to flog her because she likes it,"), as opposed a Sadist or Dominant, who might find their role a turn-on in other ways.

Sensory deprivation – depriving someone of their senses in some way. One of the ways to do so is to use blindfolds, headphones or ear plugs, a bag that provides breathing over one's head and things like that.

Scat Play – playing with feces and fecal matter.

Shibari – is a very traditional Japanese rope bondage. It's a more aesthetically specific than all the western bondage, and it uses a series of specific length and diameter ropes. In the recent ages of rope bondage, Shibari has been adapted many times and combined many more with a bit of western style, and the two are often seen and have been used together. The word itself - "Shibari" means "to tie" or "to bind."

Soft Limit – A specific element or action of play that a person isn't really comfortable with, but could be some time in the future, and/or might want to push past.

Sounding – From the medical practice, "sounding," was equivalent to "measuring," but within bodily orifices. In the modern kink word, sounding refers to the practice of inserting metal rods into the urethral openings (either on men or women).

Subdrop – An emotional, psychological, or physiological state that can sometimes come after play. It almost always involves deep feelings of loss, loneliness, abandonment, worries, misgivings about the play or one's identity as a person that's into kinkiness, and often enough the feeling of sadness. In order for one to get out of this state, it needs to be properly taken care of by doing more usual vanilla stuff like cuddling, eating and drinking favourite food and beverages (alcohol excluded).

Suspension – the practice of lifting or partially lifting the subject into the air. Most commonly seen with rope, suspension can be done with any number of things, although a familiarity with anatomy and safety practices is a must.

SSC – "Safe, Sane, and Consensual." This was one of the first acronyms to first come onto the scene, in the early 80's, that described an aware, safety-oriented kink world; an important distinction, especially before the BDSM scene was more widely accepted (or at least, more public) to differentiate between abuse and SM.

Subspace – a state of mind referring to a blissed-out, other-worldly place bottoms can go during heavy play. Subspace, also referred to as "flying," or "floating," is usually a combination of endorphins and adrenaline that, in the right mix, have an almost drug-like affect. Many bottoms report their pain tolerance sky rocketing, and a desire to keep playing forever.

S/M – originally an acronym for "Sadomasochism," S/M, SM, or S&M became an all-inclusive word meaning the same as "kink" or "BDSM," when the scene was still in its fledgling stages. Many older texts will use S/M (or "leather") in much the same way as we use "BDSM" or "kink" today.

Submissive – One who gives, relents, or doesn't have power.

Switch – One who switches between roles.

Sadist – One who enjoys giving pain.

Masochist – One who enjoys receiving pain.

Sadomasochist – One who enjoys both giving and receiving pain.

Top – a role referring to the person giving sensation. One who gives sensation or action.

Topdrop – An emotional, psychological, or physiological state than can sometimes come after play. It usually followed by feelings of loneliness, disgust, self-doubt, and general overthinking about the play or one's identity as a person with kink side of them. Things to do to get out of this state is to just focus on vanilla life things that bring happiness like cuddles, great food and possibly a great movie to watch.

Topspace – Also called "top frenzy," top space is the counterpart to subspace, and includes feelings of all-powerful euphoria and a desire to never stop.

TPE – "Total Power Exchange." This acronym refers usually to a 24/7 relationship dynamic (the two are often found in conjunction, as in, "24/7 TPE,") in which all power is exchanged, including finances and physical property.

Vanilla – A word first used to describe non-kink oriented sex, "vanilla," sometimes takes on a dismissive tone, and has come (in the some places) to mean just "boring sex." Also, a delicious ice cream flavour!

Wax Play – play involving dripping hot wax on the skin. Different waxes can be used, although many burn at different temperatures, and good research beforehand is highly recommended.

Watersports – Play involving pee, playing with pee, and peeing on one another. See also: golden showers.

Wartenberg wheel – A device originating in the medical field to test nerve ending response and sensation, the wartenberg wheel is a small, very sharp-spiked wheel that can be rolled over the skin, or used in conjunction with an electrical play unit.

Common limits include:
- blood

- disease transmission (aka unsafe sex)

- faeces/urine (also called golden showers/water sports and brown showers/scat)

- feeling claustrophobic or feeling too exposed

- feeling worthless/humiliated

- feeling unsafe or being afraid of your partner (even in a play context)

- physical marks, physical marks in some places pain, certain types of pain, pain in certain places, pain past a certain level of intensity

- triggers – anything that reminds you of a past traumatic event

Conclusion

The first and most important principle to be kept in mind when it comes to unusual behavior, as a sociological phenomenon is that "Things are not always the same as they seem at first" (Berger, 1963). In other words, the popular and generally accepted understanding of unusual behavior can be completely inaccurate. There are almost no areas of unusual behavior in which the deep gap between myth and reality can be perceived, as in sadomasochism.

First of all, pain is not a central nor a leading principle in S & M. In fact, it is not necessary for sadomasochistic activities. What is crucial is, in fact, a picture of pain, which is a symbol of domination and control. The basis of the S & M relationship is the domination and subordination, control and allowing to be controlled. It's actually far from that, the fact that pain is not part of the S & M relationship, but as such, it is a part of the very concept.

Second, the partner who is in the role of a masochist is far from passive. S&M is a social and interactive activity that involves both partners. Masochist, or subordinate partner, says his wishes to the sadist, that is, the dominant partner, what she or he wants, and what they will not do, and vice versa. Both partners are actively involved in "creating a script". Mutual cooperation, not compulsion and force, are the basis of the S & M relationship.

It's planned behavior - everything that's going on is mostly planned in advance (Gebhard 1969). This does not mean that there is no deviation from the original agreement. Limits can be negotiated, as well as the scenario itself, but the partners themselves determine the dynamics of the action before it realistically occurs. In other words, S & M is a reciprocal activity in which both partners willingly participate in an agreed scenario, in a certain part of the S & M activity, or according to Goffman terminology, within a certain framework. In 1963, Goffman wrote: "S & M is a theater, a world of transformation, a common fantasy that becomes a creation in reality, in advance of the dogmatic framework."

No study that was based on reasonably selected S & M participants showed that they were more mentally disturbed than the rest of the population. On the contrary, in studies based on nonclinical respondents, it was concluded that they are definitely normal. In the fourth volume of the American Psychiatric Association "Diagnostic and Statistical Manual of Mental Illnesses", published in 1994, a distinction was made between people who find sexual satisfaction in "real" and "simulated" beatings, humiliation and suffering.

In the end, rough sex, in which both partners are involved, is a continuation, an extension of experience and without conditioning. The degree of rudeness, obedience, control, pain - or an illusion of pain - depends solely on the agreement between partners. Moreover, for most participants in S & M, applying or receiving pain is an option, but not an obligation. In other words, sadomasochism is extreme, only in its extreme versions.

Most of those who do not want to participate in S & M, think the contrary, accordingly to the beliefs of stereotypes - if you love S & M, then you are involved in all parts, from the most basic ones to the most extreme ones. S & M is much more complex than that. The exact differences in the act and performance of certain unusual scenes and the roles that partners receive from them are the most interesting. All in all, you have to be the judge of yourself and what you want for yourself. If this is something that pleases you or can please you – try it, if not it's always good to know about it.

Copyright and Trademarks: This publication is Copyrighted 2017 by Zoodoo Publishing. All products, publications, software and services mentioned and recommended in this publication are protected by trademarks. In such instance, all trademarks & copyright belong to the respective owners. All rights reserved. No part of this book may be reproduced or transferred in any form or by any means, graphic, electronic, or mechanical, including photocopying, recording, taping, or by any information storage retrieval system, without the written permission of the authors. Pictures used in this book are either royalty free pictures bought from stock-photo websites or have the source mentioned underneath the picture.

Disclaimer and Legal Notice: This product is not legal or medical advice and should not be interpreted in that manner. You need to do your own due-diligence to determine if the content of this product is right for you. The author and the affiliates of this product are not liable for any damages or losses associated with the content in this product. While every attempt has been made to verify the information shared in this publication, neither the author nor the affiliates assume any responsibility for errors, omissions or contrary interpretation of the subject matter herein. Any perceived slights to any specific person(s) or organization(s) are purely unintentional. We have no control over the nature, content and availability of the web sites listed in this book. The inclusion of any web site links does not necessarily imply a recommendation or endorse the views expressed within them. Zoodoo Publishing takes no responsibility for, and will not be liable for, the websites being temporarily unavailable or being removed from the Internet. The accuracy and completeness of information provided herein and opinions stated herein are not guaranteed or warranted to produce any particular results, and the advice and strategies, contained herein may not be suitable for every individual. The author shall not be liable for any loss incurred as a consequence of the use and application, directly or indirectly, of any information presented in this work. This publication is designed to provide information in regards to the subject matter covered. The information included in this book has been compiled to give an overview of the subject s and detail some of the symptoms, treatments etc. that are available to people with this condition. It is not intended to give medical advice. For a firm diagnosis of your condition, and for a treatment plan suitable for you, you should consult your doctor or consultant. The writer of this book and the publisher are not responsible for any damages or negative consequences following any of the treatments or methods highlighted in this book. Website links are for informational purposes and should not be seen as a personal endorsement; the same applies to the products detailed in this book. The reader should also be aware that although the web links included were correct at the time of writing, they may become out of date in the future.

www.ingramcontent.com/pod-product-compliance
Lightning Source LLC
Chambersburg PA
CBHW061959040426
42447CB00010B/1827